The Good Confession

The Good Confession
An Exploration of the Christian Faith

Daniel R. Hyde

Wipf & Stock
PUBLISHERS
Eugene, Oregon

THE GOOD CONFESSION
An Exploration of the Christian Faith

Copyright © 2006 Daniel R. Hyde. All rights reserved. Except for brief quotations in critical articles or reviews, no part of this book may be reproduced in any manner without prior written permission from the publisher. Write: Permissions, Wipf & Stock Publishers, 199 W. 8th Ave., Suite 3, Eugene, OR 97401.

ISBN 10: 1-59752-869-2
ISBN 13: 978-1-59752-869-6

Manufactured in the U.S.A.

Unless otherwise indicated, all Scripture quotations are from The Holy Bible, English Standard Version, copyright © 2001 by Crossway Bibles, a division of Good News Publishers. Used by permission. All rights reserved.

To the
Oceanside United Reformed Church

"I will most gladly spend and be spent for your souls."
(2 Cor 12:15)

Contents

Introduction / 1
Using This Book / 3

1. A "Confessional" Church / 7
2. The Attributes of God / 29
3. Knowing God in His Word / 35
4. The Holy Trinity / 51
5. Creation and Providence / 63
6. The Creation and Fall of Humanity / 71
7. Election / 81
8. The Covenant of Grace / 87
9. Jesus Christ / 93
10. The Death of Christ / 101
11. Justification / 111
12. Sanctification / 117
13. Preservation/Perseverance / 129
14. The Church: Part 1 / 135
15. The Church: Part 2 / 149
16. The Sacraments / 157
17. The Return of Christ and Heaven / 173
18. Understanding and Enjoying Worship / 177

Introduction

THIS BOOK is for pilgrims who cry out in the words of the hymn, "Guide me, O Thou great Jehovah, pilgrim through this barren land." A pilgrim is one that is seeking a permanent home. As Christians, we know that our ultimate home will be in the presence of God in the new creation (Rev 21–22); yet, as pilgrims in this life, the church of Jesus Christ acts as our "home away from home" (e.g., Eph 2) until we "tread the verge of Jordan."

In this workbook, we will be exploring the meaning of being a Christian. Some already know what this means, others have forgotten, while some have never had it explained to them. So that we will all be able to confess with the Body of Christ the "good confession" (1 Tim 6:12), we will explore what it means to be a Christian together. In sum, to be a Christian is to join the great "cloud of witnesses" (Heb 12:1) through the ages, confessing with them the "faith that was once for all delivered to the saints" (Jude 3). For this reason we are not going to explore recent fads or strange new doctrines unheard of in the history of the Church. Instead, we will be studying what it means to be a "Christian" from the vantage point of the Bible as well as the early church creeds and Protestant confessions.

May God, by his Spirit, use this feeble workbook in leading you to understand, affirm, and whole-heartedly trust in the beautiful doctrines of God's Word, so that you too can join in making "the good confession:"

Make me to know your ways, O LORD; teach me your paths.

Lead me in your truth and teach me. (Ps 25:4–5)

Using This Book

Ways This Book Can Be Used Effectively

Membership/Inquirers Class

If you are using this workbook as a membership/inquirers class, the teacher/leader is encouraged to read my article, "Teaching Membership Classes." *Ordained Servant* 14:1 (March 2005): 11–14.[1]

Adult Sunday School/Catechism

Since most adult Sunday School classes are taught by those without much time, energy, and resources, this workbook allows a teacher in such a situation to focus on content rather than presentation, since it is already organized.

Bible Study

I designed this workbook for personal reflection and corporate interaction. It is, therefore, suited for a small-group Bible study. Related to this would be using the book in this way along with inquiring neighbors who may be interested to learn what Christianity is all about.

Personal Study

If you are seeking a way of personal enrichment in the basics of the Christian Faith, this workbook is an effective, structured means to do that as well.

---

[1] *Ordained Servant* may be found at http://opc.org/os_archive.html.

Using This Book

Several Suggested "Tracks"

In my experience, all classes are different. Who is in the class should lead to reflection on the pace and amount of material in a single class session.

If you are using this book as a Sunday school class or Bible study as a season-long curriculum, then simply follow the chapters in their order.

If you are using this book as a "membership/inquirers" class among people who are coming to your church with a good grasp of basic Christian doctrine, a shorter, overview type of class such as the following would suffice:

6–Sessions (2 hours each session)

    Week 1—Lesson 1

    Week 2—Lessons 3 and 5

    Week 3—Lessons 8 and 9

    Week 4—Lesson 11

    Week 5—Lesson 14

    Week 6—Lesson 16

If you are using this book as a "membership/inquirers" class and there are many young Christians, people new to the Reformed Faith, or even non-Christian inquirers, then a longer, more intensive course is called for such as:

12–Sessions (1 hour each session)

    Week 1—Lesson 1

    Week 2—Lesson 2

    Week 3—Lesson 3

    Week 4—Lessons 4 and 5

    Week 5—Lesson 6

    Week 6—Lessons 7 and 8

Using This Book

Week 7—Lessons 9 and 10

Week 8—Lesson 11

Week 9—Lesson 12 and 13

Week 10—Lesson 14 and 15

Week 11—Lesson 16 and 17

Week 12—Lesson 18

Undoubtedly there are many other settings to use this book and many other methods of presenting its material. This is why it is so important to know your audience and their level of understanding and comprehension before moving on.

1

A "Confessional" Church

REFLECTION QUESTION

What do you believe as a Christian?
How do you summarize your faith when asked?

Faith Seeking Understanding

"I BELIEVE, IN order to understand; and I understand, the better to believe." These words of the great church father Augustine of Hippo (A.D. 354–430) summarize not only a philosophical belief in the relationship between faith and knowledge, but also the ordinary pilgrim's lifelong pursuit of knowing and worshipping God.

For many of us, first trusting in Jesus Christ was very simple: "God, be merciful to me, a sinner" (Luke 18:13). Although we had a basic knowledge of who Jesus was and who we are, we believed and then began to understand. But now as believers in the Lord Jesus Christ, whether young or old, we are called to pursue the Lord with all that we are, loving him with our hearts, our souls, *and* our minds (Matt 22:37). Our simple faith gave birth to an increasing knowledge of the Lord and his Word, which now continues to strengthen our faith.

Not only is this true of each of us individually, but this is also true corporately of the Church, not only here and now, but throughout the ages of history. One of the ways the Christian Church has expressed her knowledge and faith through the centuries is in the great creeds and confessions.[1] In order for our faith to seek understanding, let us take a few moments to discuss what creeds and confessions are in the life and history of the Christian Church and in the life of the Christian. The creeds and confessions are the expression of the Church's faith, and by studying them, we grow in our knowledge and love of the Lord.

"But our church has no creed but Christ!"[2] No doubt, you too have heard this from many Christians or have said it yourself. This bumper-sticker type slogan has virtually become a part of what it means to be Christian in contemporary churches.

Have you ever stopped to think about what this statement means, though? This slogan is actually one of the most ironic statements anyone can make. You see, when a person or even a church states that they have "no creed but Christ," they are ironically, in fact, making a "creed," a "confession of faith." To say, "I have no creed," is itself a creed! What we as Christians need to understand is that this is not a biblical way of thinking or acting, but in fact, shows that Christians have been influenced by modern philosophy. When someone makes the statement, "I have no creed but Christ," he is actually falling into the trap of popular modern philosophy, when it says, "There is no absolute truth;" for, the statement, "There is no absolute truth" is itself a statement of absolute truth!

---

[1] I use the feminine pronoun "her" for the Church because the Scriptures speak this way. For example, Paul says, "Husbands, loves your wives, as Christ loved the church and gave himself up for her, that he might sanctify her, having cleansed her . . . that she might be holy and without blemish" (Eph. 5:25–27). John also speaks this way, saying, "And I saw the holy city, new Jerusalem, coming down out of heaven from God, prepared as a bride adorned for her husband" (Rev 21:2). See also Ps 46:4–5, 48:12–14, 87:5, 102:13–16, 132:13–16; Isa 49, 50, 54, 66:7ff; Jer 3, 4; Gal 4:26; Rev 12:17, 19:7.

[2] This slogan comes from the separatist group known as the Disciples of Christ (or, "Campbellites"), which was founded in 1809 by Thomas Campbell, a Presbyterian preacher who tried to gather scattered groups of Christians on the basis of nothing but "the primitive and simple gospel." After this another Presbyterian minister, Barton Warren Stone, broke away from the church and formed a group called the "Christians." Similar separatist groups left the Methodist church under the leadership of James O'Kelley and the Baptist church under Abner Jones and Elias Smith. In 1832 Stone's group and many from the other groups united as the "Disciples." A separation into two churches took place in 1906 because of a dispute over the use of instrumental music in worship; those who allowed them became known as the Disciples of Christ and those who did not the Churches of Christ. In 1968 the Disciples of Christ were renamed the Christian Church.

A "Confessional" Church

Therefore, from the outset of this short study, let us all agree that everyone, including Christians and churches, have some system of belief behind what they say. Whether they speak of believing a particular creed or confession of faith or none at all, they all have a theology and way of thinking. So whether you as an individual Christian have actually thought through what your "theology" is, or whether a church has actually written down what they believe in a statement of faith, the fact remains true—all of us have creeds and a way of thinking and explaining that creed. As a very simplistic example of this, consider the following dialog:

Me: What does your church believe?

You: We believe the Bible, and the Bible *only*.

Me: So what does the Bible teach?

You: The main thing it teaches is who Jesus Christ is.

Me: So, who is this "Jesus Christ?"

You: He is God's Son and our Savior.

Me: So why do I need to know about him?

You: Because to be saved you must believe in him.

Me: "To be saved?" Saved from what?

You: Your sin.

Me: Why do I need to be saved from my sin?

You: Because it separates you from God and leads to eternal death.

As you can imagine, we can keep going on and on in this dialog, but I hope you see the point it makes. Anytime you explain simply to a friend what you believe, whether he is a believer or an unbeliever, you are confessing your creed; you are confessing your faith in a way that explains how you understand the Bible. No human has a mind that is a *tabula rasa*, that is, a "blank slate." None of us reads and explains the Bible without any interaction with our own personality, ability to read and interpret, our life experiences, and our personal beliefs. Instead, all of us must explain the Bible when someone asks us what it believes.

Therefore, all of us need to have the Bible explained to us so that we know what it teaches in the first place.

What Are Creeds and Confessions?

Since we all have a personal creed and a way of confessing our faith to the world, this shows us that creeds and confessions of faith are not bad things. We should not let the word "creed" frighten us. Therefore, when you hear a pastor or member of a church say, "We believe the *Apostles' Creed*," or, "We believe what the *Heidelberg Catechism* teaches," do not think this means that we are somehow part of the Roman Catholic Church.

Instead, to be a "confessional church" is to be a church that believes and confesses the Word of God as summarized in the great creeds and confessions of the historic Church; it is to be a church firmly rooted in the Scriptures. From the very beginning of Israel's life as a community through its maturation in the New Testament church, the people of God have confessed what they believe with brief summaries of the Faith. We call these summaries "creeds and confessions."

Before the label "Roman Catholic" came to be what it is in our understanding, believers in the LORD and in Jesus Christ had creeds and confessions. Our English word "creed" is a literal translation of the Latin word *credo*, which means, "I believe." A "confession" is a more detailed explanation of the Christian Faith, and this word also comes from a Latin root, meaning, "I publicly declare." Notice how saying "I believe" involves knowing something, speaking something, and trusting something despite the world's discouragement. As one writer says,

> Believing is an act of one's whole being and personality. A person believes with the mind, the heart, and the will. Believing includes knowledge, passion, and commitment. It is an act of the whole person.[3]

We are a confessional church. This means that we all believe in our hearts and confess with our mouths the teaching of God's holy Word, the Bible, and express what we believe that Word to teach in time-tested, written documents that we call the "creeds" and "confessions" of the Christian Church.

---

[3] John H. Leith, *The Church: A Believing Community* (Atlanta: John Knox, 1981), 68.

A "Confessional" Church

Reflection Question

What advantages are there for a church in having its confession/beliefs made known?

Where Are Creeds & Confessions in the Bible?

Before we discuss these creeds and confessions, let us answer the question, "Are creeds and confessions biblical?" We have assumed so far that they are, but for our benefit let us examine why we believe they are biblical and where we find them in the Bible.

The practice of writing out summary statements of the Faith, which lives in the hearts and is confessed by the mouths of God's people, is as old as the Church itself. We find in both the Old and New Testaments of the Holy Scriptures basic summary statements of the Faith of God's people.

Old Testament

In the Old Testament, the people of God were like a little child confessing their faith in a very simple way. The primary confession of faith of Israel is what is called the *Shema*, which is the Hebrew word for "hear." We find the *Shema* in Deuteronomy 6:4, which says, "Hear, O Israel, the LORD our God: the LORD is one!" These words were recited every morning and evening by God's people (Deut 6:7).

Understand also the context in which the LORD gave this confession of faith to Israel: their *exodus* out of Egypt. After leaving the "house of slavery" (Exod 20:2), the LORD saved Israel from the armies of Egypt by leading them through the Red Sea on dry ground (Exod 14:22). After this climactic display of the LORD's power in salvation and judgment, the LORD spoke his words to Moses, who then wrote them down for the people of God. In Deuteronomy 6, we have Moses' command to the people of God to express their faith and commitment in the LORD by reciting this brief, radical creed. It was radical because they had just come out of Egypt, which had many "gods," and they were about to enter the land of the Canaanites, who had many "gods" themselves. So it was in the midst of false religion and idolatry that the Israelites confessed to the nations around them, that the LORD alone was "God of gods" and "Lord of lords" (Ps 136:2–3), while the "gods" of the nations were merely "silver and gold, the work of men's hands" (Ps 115:4).

Another confession of faith of the LORD's people is found in Deuteronomy 26:1–11, which says,

> [1]When you come into the land that the LORD your God is giving you for an inheritance and have taken possession of it and live in it, [2]you shall take some of the first of all the fruit of the ground, which you harvest from your land that the LORD your God is giving you, and you shall put it in a basket, and you shall go to the place that the LORD your God will choose, to make his name to dwell there. [3]And you shall go to the priest who is in office at that time and say to him, "I declare today to the LORD your God that I have come into the land that the LORD swore to our fathers to give us." [4]Then the priest shall take the basket from your hand and set it down before the altar of the LORD your God. [5]And you shall make response before the LORD your God,
>
> "A wandering Aramean was my father. And he went down into Egypt and sojourned there, few in number, and there he became a nation, great, mighty, and populous. [6]And the Egyptians treated us harshly and humiliated us and laid on us hard labor. [7]Then we cried to the LORD, the God of our fathers, and the LORD heard our voice and saw our affliction, our toil, and our oppression. [8]And the LORD brought us out of Egypt with a mighty hand and an outstretched arm, with great deeds of terror, with signs and wonders. [9]And he brought us into this place and gave us this land, a land flowing with milk and honey. [10]And behold, now I bring the first of the fruit of the ground, which you, O LORD, have given me."
>
> And you shall set it down before the LORD your God and worship before the LORD your God. [11]And you shall rejoice in all the good that the LORD your God has given to you and to your house, you, and the Levite, and the sojourner who is among you.

Notice that this was a declaration when publicly worshipping the LORD in response to his blessings of salvation. What God had done in history, his people believed and confessed.

A "Confessional" Church

REFLECTION QUESTIONS

When the people of God confessed and recited the *Shema*, what was it teaching them?

From what errors was the *Shema* protecting the people of God?

As you read the Old Testament, write down any other creedal statements you come across.

New Testament

With the coming of the Son of God in human flesh in the birth of our Lord Jesus Christ in "the fullness of time" (Gal 4:4), the people of God reached an age of maturity. Therefore, the creeds and confessions that we read throughout the New Testament are many in number, and a fuller expression of the belief of God's people.

The primary New Testament confession of faith is Peter's statement, "You are the Christ, the Son of the Living God" (Matt 16:16). Peter's confession of Jesus consists of two points. First, Jesus is "the Christ," that is, he is the Messiah, the anointed One. In the Old Testament, there were three anointed "offices"—prophet, priest, and king. These anointed ones were the leaders of Israel. Therefore, when Peter calls Jesus "*the* Christ," he is confessing that he is the final anointed prophet, priest, and king of God's people and the One promised and hoped for in the Old Testament. In addition, as the Messiah, he is the Savior of his people.

Second, Jesus is confessed to be "the Son of the Living God." To be "*the* Son" of God means that Jesus Christ is eternal with God, that is, he is God!

Reflection Questions

What do Jesus' words in Matthew 16:15 (cf. Matt 10:32) tell us about his attitude toward confessing our faith?

What does Peter's creed confess about Christ, especially in light of the Old Testament?

Later on in the life of the Church, as the good news of Jesus Christ began spreading into the Gentile world, the Apostles gave the Church fuller creeds and confessions. Because they would soon die, the Apostles gave these more detailed creeds and confessions to the Church to record their teaching for generations to come.

Thus in 1 Corinthians 15:3–4 Paul passes down the truths he received, "That Christ died for our sins according to the Scriptures, and that he was buried, and that he rose again the third day according to the Scriptures."

Notice that Paul says this creed was not his own, but it had been passed down to him. One generation passes down the Christian Faith to another as a witness of what God has done. This is one of the reasons the historic Christian Church has included a confession of faith in public worship from the earliest of days of the Church.

Paul also says he passed down the simple gospel: Christ's death, burial, and resurrection. Moreover, these events of history were "according to the Scriptures," that is, the Old Testament. Creeds, therefore, are not our own opinions, but a testimony of what God has done in sending his Son Jesus Christ.

A "Confessional" Church

The Epistle to the Ephesians is *the* epistle of the Church since its main theme is ecclesiology, the doctrine of the Church. In Ephesians 4:4–6, Paul records what scholars understand as a creed that a new convert to Christianity recited at baptism. Notice that this creedal statement speaks in very broad terms, saying, "There is one body . . . one Spirit . . . one hope . . . one Lord . . . one faith . . . one baptism . . . one God and Father."

The most striking thing about this creed is that there are seven articles, or points of faith. Seven, of course, is the biblical number that oftentimes signifies completion. What we have in this creed, then, is the Christian Faith in summary.

As well, this creed confesses that this truth unites us. Unlike the popular slogan which says, "Doctrine divides," creeds are not meant to divide the Body of Christ, but they are in fact unifying statements. Notice that the creed in Ephesians 4:4–6 confesses that there is *one* body, *one* Spirit, etc. They give us all a common expression of our faith so that we will be like-minded and unified in our love for the Lord.

A final example of a New Testament creed are the words of 1 Timothy 3:16. Paul's words as recorded in First and Second Timothy were among his last. He wrote to Timothy, the young pastor of the church in Ephesus. Paul desired to visit him (3:14), but until he came, he wanted Timothy to understand how to live within the household of God (3:15). First Timothy, then, is a kind of church order, that is, a rule book on how to pray, worship, teach, lead, choose elders and deacons, minister to widows, the rich, the poor, etc. In 1 Timothy 3:16 Paul says,

> And *confessedly* great is the mystery of piety:
> Who was manifested in the flesh,
> justified in the Spirit,
> seen by angels,
> preached among the Gentiles,
> believed on in the world,
> received up in glory. (author's translation)

Paul actually begins this creed with a preface, using the Greek work for "confession," which I have translated as "confessedly." Notice also that this confession of faith is not merely for the mind, but for our lives. "Piety" is the believers' reverent response to God in all areas of his life as he/she seeks to show his/her gratitude. Creeds are utterly practical and devotional for us as Christians as they guide us in our thoughts about God and our prayers to God. This creed is a devotional aid for our piety because it focuses our hearts and minds upon the work of our Lord Jesus Christ. The individual lines move from Christ's Incarnation to his resurrection, to his Ascension, to his present ministry through proclamation, to his being the object of faith, and finally to his present reign at the right hand of the Father.

These texts of Scripture, both from the Old and New Testament, show us that creeds and confessions are not only what stuffy, "dead orthodox" churches have, or only what "Catholics" believe. Instead, Christians throughout the generations have written and recited creeds to express the faith that lives in their hearts.

Reflection Question

How did the creed of 1 Timothy 3:16 function in the church at Ephesus, especially in light of the fact that Paul had yet to arrive there?

What About *Sola Scriptura*?

"But don't creeds and confessions contradict the Protestant belief in *sola Scriptura*, 'Scripture alone?'" While creeds and confessions can usurp the place of Scripture in a persons' life or the life of a church, we do not believe that just by having creeds and confessions we are placing them in Scriptures' place.

Reflection

Write out what you think the Protestant slogan *sola Scriptura* means.

A "Confessional" Church

There are several reasons for saying that the creeds and confessions do not take the place of the Scriptures in a confessional church.

First, *sola Scriptura* means that Scripture alone is the only God-given rule for faith and life, doctrine and practice, what we believe and how we live. The inspired Word of God judges and rules our creeds and confessions.

Second, the Protestant confession of *sola Scriptura* does not mean that we do not need any help in understanding the Scriptures. We live in an individualistic generation. In Christian circles this expresses itself in a "me and my Bible" type of attitude. We live in a time in which everyone does what is right in his own eyes when reading and interpreting the Scriptures (cf. Judg 21:25). We must not forget that God, in his infinite wisdom, has established a visible Church, and that in the Church he has ordained pastors and teachers throughout the history of the Church to expound and interpret the meaning of Scripture to the Church. As we said earlier, even a person who says "I have no creed" and, "I just read the Bible," ends up interpreting Scripture according to his or her own particular beliefs. Creeds and confessions limit our selfishness and unite our hearts in unselfishness to the Church that has existed throughout the ages.

Third, our creeds and confessions are not inspired, nor do we make this claim. Their authority and doctrinal purity comes from the inspired source of sacred Scripture alone. This means that they have a derived authority, which comes from Scripture alone. Because of this, we believe what our creeds and confessions teach because they agree with the Word of God. If they are unbiblical, the Church must change them.

REFLECTION QUESTION

What role can/should creeds and
confessions play in our day?

Are Creeds and Confessions Necessary?

The early Church needed creeds and confessions. Jesus command his people to confess their faith, saying, "Therefore everyone who confesses Me before men, I will also confess him before My Father who is in heaven" (Matt 10:32; NASB). As well, the Apostle Paul said, "If you confess with your mouth that Jesus is Lord and believe in your heart that God raised him from the dead, you will be saved. For with the heart one believes and is justified, and with the mouth one confesses and is saved" (Rom 10:9–10).

When the Apostles died and the Church was busy fulfilling Jesus' command to "go into all the nations" (Matt 28:19), there were two extremely urgent needs that confronted the confessing Church.

First, all the new converts to Christianity had to be taught the Christian Faith so that they could declare their allegiance to Jesus Christ. They had to be "catechized." This word comes from the Greek verb *katēcheō*, which occurs eight times in the New Testament.[4] It is a compound Greek word from *kata*, "down," and *ēcheō*, "sound;" thus meaning, "I sound down." Catechism is teaching with questions and answers. Sometimes we call this the "Socratic method" of instruction. The early Church needed a basic way to guide new members of Christ's Church into knowledge of what they believed. In the early church the basic outline of "new members classes" were the *Apostles' Creed*, the Sacraments, the Lord's Prayer, and the Ten Commandments,

Second, the early Church had to stand strong in the Faith of the Scriptures against many "heresies," or false teachings. To confront and reject false teaching, the earliest churches gathered to write, for example, the *Nicene Creed*. Since representatives from the whole Church in those

---

[4] In the New Testament, Luke uses this word four times as does Paul. Luke uses it in Acts 21:21 and 21:24 in a general sense of "informed." He also uses it of specific teaching in the Christian Faith. In Acts 18:25 we learn about Apollos, who "had been instructed (*katēchēmenos*) in the way of the Lord." Luke also uses this word in the prologue to his Gospel, written to Theophilus, "that you may have certainty concerning the things you have been taught" (*katēchēthēs*; Luke 1:4). Paul uses this verb exclusively for religious instruction. Paul uses it of the instruction the Jews received in Romans 2:18: "you are instructed (*katēchoumenos*) from the law." In addition, he uses it for the instruction Christians receive, what we call "catechizing." First Corinthians 14:19 says, " . . . in church I would rather speak five words with my mind in order to instruct (*katēchēsō*) others, than ten thousand words in a tongue." Finally, he speaks in Galatians 6:6, saying, "One who is taught (*katēchoumenos*, i.e., "the one catechized" or "the catechumen") the word must share all good things with the one who teaches" (*katēchounti*, i.e., "catechizes").

days gathered to write this creed, it is an "ecumenical" creed. The word "ecumenical" simply means "general" or "universal." The whole Church wrote them, and the whole Church believed them.

In our day and age, creeds and confessions are even more necessary than ever. Over 100 years ago, J. C. Ryle spoke the following words, which are prophetic of our day:

> The tendency of modern thought is to reject dogmas, creeds and every kind of bounds in religion. It is thought grand and wise to condemn no opinion whatsoever, and to pronounce all earnest and clever teachers to be trustworthy, however heterogeneous and mutually destructive their opinions may be. Everything forsooth is true, and nothing is false! Everybody is right and nobody is wrong! Everybody is likely to be saved and nobody is to be lost![5]

A Brief Overview of the Ecumenical Creeds

Reformed churches, then, do not teach novel doctrines, but are historic Christian churches. Because of this, they join with the ancient Christian church in confessing the ecumenical creeds of the ancient Church: the *Apostles'*, *Nicene*, and *Athanasian Creeds* and *Definition of Chalcedon*.

Apostles' Creed

The *Apostles' Creed* was not written by the Apostles themselves, but was developed over time by the ancient churches (A.D. 100–700). We call it the *Apostles' Creed* because all the phrases come straight out of the doctrine of the Apostles in the Scriptures. The first official version of what would later become the *Apostles' Creed* was used in Rome in the 2nd century as a way to instruct converts who were preparing for baptism (cf. Eph 4:4–6).

The *Apostles' Creed* confesses in a basic way that the Christian believes there is one God who exists in three persons. We call this the doctrine of the Holy Trinity. In doing this, the *Creed* has three simple parts. In the first part we confess to believe in God the Father, our Creator; in the second part we confess to believe in Jesus Christ, our Redeemer; and in the third part we confess to believe in the Holy Spirit, our Sanctifier.

---

[5] J. C. Ryle, *Holiness: Its Nature, Hindrances, Difficulties, & Roots* (1879; Moscow, ID: Charles Nolan Publishers, reprinted 2001), 13.

Nicene Creed

The *Nicene Creed* was first written in A.D. 325 at the first ecumenical Council of Nicea, a city in modern-day Turkey. Representatives from throughout the Church gathered to respond to and reject the false teaching of a preacher named Arius. Arius taught that the Son of God was not eternal, but was the first creation of God the Father. What this meant was that Jesus Christ was less divine than God the Father. Later, at the second ecumenical Council of Constantinople in 381, the churches responded to the false teaching of the Macedonians who said that the Holy Spirit was not fully God. Thus, the phrases about the Holy Spirit in the *Nicene Creed* were added to complete this great creed. Because of its depth of teaching and purpose in protecting the Church, the *Nicene Creed* is the most important of the Christian creeds.[6]

In the *Nicene Creed*, we confess to believe in God the Father, God the Son, and God the Holy Spirit, as well as confess the Church of Christ.

Athanasian Creed

The *Athanasian Creed* is named after St. Athanasius (A.D. 296–373), a deacon in the church in Alexandria, Egypt. Athanasius was one of the staunchest opponents of the teachings of Arius at the Council of Nicea. Like the *Apostles' Creed*, the *Athanasian Creed* was most likely not written by its namesake, but was taken from his writings against Arius. These different parts of his writings were later compiled into a beautifully poetic creed sometime between A.D. 500–800. It is divided into two parts. The first part confesses a detailed explanation of the doctrine of the Trinity, that we believe and worship one God in Unity and Unity in Trinity. In the second part, it confesses a detailed explanation of the doctrine of the Person of Christ, that there is one Lord Jesus Christ, who is both perfect God and perfect man. Both of these parts of the creed open with a statement of the necessity to believe in the Triune nature of God and two natures of Christ to have salvation.

Definition of Chalcedon

The *Definition of Chalcedon* was written in A.D. 451 at the fourth ecumenical council of Chalcedon, a modern-day city in Turkey. At this

---

[6] Leith, *The Church*, 87.

council, the churches of the ancient world gathered to respond to several different false teachings about who our Lord Jesus Christ is.

One false teaching was Nestorianism, which taught that Christ's two "natures"—his divinity and humanity—were divided so that Christ was two completely separate Persons and not united in the one Person of Christ. Another heresy was that of Eutychianism, which taught that Christ's natures were so united in his Person, that the divine nature swallowed up the human nature, thus leaving one mixed nature. The third heresy was Apollinarianism, which taught that Jesus had a true human body and a "lower soul" (which animals have), but that the eternal *logos* (the "Word" of John 1:1) replaced the "higher soul" (which only humans have). This meant that Jesus Christ was not as fully human as we are.

Again, theologians, pastors, and church leaders had to meet to respond to false teaching and confess what the Word of God taught on this vital doctrine of Christ. The *Definition* is one paragraph in which the Church confesses to believe in *one* Lord Jesus Christ, who has two natures, a divine and a human.

A Brief Overview of the Three Forms of Unity

As a Christian church, we confess the ancient Christian creeds. Later in the history of the church, the great Protestant Reformation occurred. During this time, it was necessary again to catechize and protect the Church against false teaching. Because of the doctrinal errors of the Roman Catholic Church, various theologians, pastors, and groups of churches wrote simple explanations of the Faith in catechisms and explained this Faith in much more detailed fashion in confessions. These instructed Christians in what the Holy Scriptures truly taught as well as to protect these new "Protestant" Christians from the many theological errors of those days. Reformed churches confess to believe the "Three Forms of Unity": the *Belgic Confession, Heidelberg Catechism,* and *Canons of Dort*. We speak of the *Three Forms* of Unity because there are three *forms*, or formulas, expressing our beliefs (*Heidelberg Catechism, Belgic Confession, Canons of Dort*). We speak of the Three Forms of *Unity* because these confessions, like all creeds, unify us in heart, soul, mind, and strength in what we believe the Word of God teaches.

Belgic Confession

Guido de Brès, a Reformed pastor in the Netherlands, published the *Belgic Confession* in 1561. He wrote this confession on behalf of the persecuted Reformed churches throughout the Netherlands (now Holland, Belgium, and N. France) as an explanation of the Reformed Faith to the Roman Catholic King of Spain, Philip II, who also ruled over the Netherlands. Its purpose was to demonstrate that the Reformed Christians were not trying to overthrow the government, as the radical "Anabaptists," but that Reformation theology was simply the faith of the ancient church. This *Confession* is as inspiring for what it says just as much as it is for the attitude of those Reformed Christians who confessed it. In an adjoining letter to the King, the Reformed Christians said that they were ready to "offer their backs to stripes, their tongues to knives, their mouths to gags, and their whole bodies to fire," rather than deny what was contained in this writing.

What the *Belgic Confession* teaches is basic Christian doctrine, organized in a very understandable way. The *Confession* has six major parts:

1. What we confess about God (arts. 1–13)
2. What we confess about Man (arts. 14–15)
3. What we confess about Christ (arts. 16–21)
4. What we confess about Salvation (arts. 22–26)
5. What we confess about the Church (arts. 27–36)
6. What we confess about the End (art. 37)

Heidelberg Catechism

The *Heidelberg Catechism* was published in 1563 in Heidelberg, Germany at the request of Fredrick III, ruler of the region of Germany called the Palatinate, in order to instruct his people in the Reformation's teachings. The two primary authors were Zacharius Ursinus, a twenty-eight year old professor of theology, and Caspar Olevianus, a twenty-six year old preacher at the Holy Ghost Church, in the center of Heidelberg.

At first, it was intended solely for the region of the Palatinate, but quickly underwent several editions and became the most popular, widely used, and comforting catechism of the Reformation period. It was even the first explanation of Reformed theology used in America when immigrants came here several hundred years ago.

A "Confessional" Church

The *Catechism* explains the Christian Faith in three parts, following the outline of the book of Romans. After questions 1–2 open with the theme (Christian comfort and confidence) and outline of the *Catechism*, the rest of the *Catechism* is outlined in this way:

Guilt/*Sin* (Q&A 3–11; Rom 1:18–3:20)

Grace/*Salvation* (Q&A 12–85; Rom 3:21–11:36)

Gratitude/*Service* (Q&A 86–129; Rom 12–16).

Canons of Dort

The last of our confessions are the *Canons of Dort*, written in 1618–19 in Dordrecht, Holland. After the Reformed Faith established itself in the Netherlands, a great controversy arose with the church there. A teacher of theology at the University of Leiden, James Arminius, and his followers, the "Arminians," were teaching new doctrines:

1. that God chose man to salvation from eternity because he saw man choosing him

2. that Jesus Christ died for all the sins of every human being

3. that a person was free enough to reject the almighty work of the Holy Spirit, even if the Holy Spirit came to save him

4. that a person who was born again could lose their salvation.

Because of this teaching, a "Synod," that is, a church gathering, was called with the pastors and theologians in the Netherlands, as well as from throughout Europe. Of this Synod, the great English Puritan John Owen said, "The divines of that assembly . . . were esteemed of the best that all the reformed churches of Europe (that of France excepted) could afford."

The result of this Synod was the rejection of Arminianism in the *Canons of Dort*. A "canon" is simply a "rule." The *Canons of Dort*, then, are the rules of faith of the Synod of Dort. The *Canons* are the official teaching of the Reformed churches on what are commonly call the "Five Points of Calvinism," or, "TULIP." It is important to note, though, that they are a response to certain teachings and not a full expression of the Reformed Faith. That is why we have the *Belgic Confession* and *Heidelberg Catechism*. The teaching of the *Canons of Dort* is divided into four parts:

1. Unconditional Election
2. Limited Atonement
3. Man's Total Depravity and God's Irresistible Grace
4. Preservation/Perseverance of the Saints

So as a Christian and Reformed church, we believe and confess to the world these particular creeds and confessions because their teachings come straight from the Bible and they have been believed by Christians for many centuries.

How Are These Creeds and Confessions Practically Used?

Besides the above reasons for believing these creeds and confessions, there are also several practical reasons for believing these statements of the Faith, which have an effect on our identity as a congregation.

They Are the Basis for Our Fellowship

The practical effect of these creeds and confessions is church unity. The Church of the Lord Jesus Christ is not a divided collection of individual, lone-ranger Christians, or individual parts, but is a single, united body in which each individual member is united in their faith. Although we are many, we are one body in Christ (Rom 12:5). As members of a Reformed church, we all confess the same Faith in matters of essentials. We see in the New Testament the apostle Paul praying for unity to become increasingly true within the churches. He prays that we would be "like-minded toward one another" and that we "may with one mind and one mouth glorify the God and Father of our Lord Jesus Christ" (Rom 15:5–6). Elsewhere he calls us to action, saying, " . . . stand fast in one spirit, with one mind striving together for the faith of the gospel" (Phil 1:27).

They Are Teaching Aids

Another practical aspect of these creeds and confessions is that we use them as a basis for our teaching, from the earliest age of children in Sunday school and at home, to teaching adults to be prepared to give an answer for the hope that is within them. (1 Pet 3:15)

The New Testament teaches the necessity of having a unified theology because the people of God are always tempted to "turn aside to fables" (2 Tim 4:4) and be "tossed to and fro and carried about with every wind of doctrine" (Eph 4:14). Instead, we are called to hold on to the "pattern of sound words" (2 Tim 1:13), the "form of doctrine . . . once for all delivered to the saints" (Rom 6:17; Jude 3), and the "whole counsel of God" (Acts 20:27).

Within the Church, the Lord has given the responsibility to pastors and elders to heed our Lord's words to teach disciples "all things that I have commanded you" (Matt 28:19–20). We are to do this from the earliest age with our children, teaching the things "we have heard and known, and our fathers have told us." As the Psalmist goes on to say, we are not to "hide them from [our] children," but are to declare

> to the generation to come the praises of the LORD, and his strength and his wonderful works that he has done . . . that [we] should make them known to [our] children, that the generation to come might know them, the children who would be born, that they may arise and declare them to their children. (Ps 78:1–6)

They Protect the Flock from Heresy

Because the Church has always existed in the midst of perilous times, her members need protection from wolves by her shepherds. As Paul warns young pastor Timothy, in these "latter times" (1 Tim 4:1) false teachers will come. Therefore, the apostle John calls us to be discerning and to "test the spirits, whether they are from God, because many false prophets have gone out into the world" (1 John 4:1).

The Church, then, is a doctrinal institution and people. John does not call us to test the spirits by the numerical and financial results a teacher or church has, nor by how charismatic and out-going a teachers' personality is. We must test the spirits by examining a doctrinal confession (1 John 4:1–3; 1 Tim 4). Paul commanded the elders of the church in Ephesus to examine doctrine, saying, "Savage wolves will come in among you, not sparing the flock . . . speaking perverse things, to draw away the disciples" (Acts 20:29–30).

By believing and confessing a clear, systematic, and comprehensive system of truth, we are less likely to see our sheep drawn away. This also equips the elders to better warn and protect the sheep of Christ. Thus, an elder is to "hold fast the faithful word as he has been taught, that he may be able, by sound doctrine, both to exhort and convict those who contradict" (Titus 1:9).

They Provide a Public Standard for Church Discipline

Summaries of the Christian Faith in creeds and confessions also provide an object standard by which the Church is to discipline those in error, whether doctrinal or ethical. This is eminently practical in our day in which too many churches have sprung up from a person's desire to be a pastor and in which people flock to a church based on feelings, preferences, and "successful" ministries. What happens in these types of churches is that the pastor is a pope and there is no accountability structure except "what the pastor says, goes." Thus, people are excommunicated, dis-fellowshipped, and shunned without any biblical steps of reconciliation, simply because of personal differences or not agreeing with the pastor.

In a Reformed church this is not so. For example, if a member should stray from the truth, other members and the elders have a way of objectively identifying their error. Remember, since everyone says, "I believe the Bible," the creeds and confessions give a summary of the Word as well as an explanation on difficult points of doctrine. For the welfare of the wayward believer as well as the entire congregation, the elders hold an erring member accountable. The same holds true for ethical error within the church. Church discipline, then, is not a case of the pastor versus someone teaching contrary to his doctrine, of a person who sins being immediately kicked out, but it is a loving process, clearly delineating between truth and error (Rom 16:17).

They Provide a Standard to Evaluate Teaching

The above description of discipline holds true for the pastor as well. The pastor is a servant of Christ; he is not untouchable. How, then, does a member of a church identify error in a church? By comparing the official teaching of the church to what is taught. The confessions, then, keep a pastor from straying into his own ideas or novel doctrines. He must be careful to teach and preach only the apostolic doctrine that has been handed down to him, and to "commit these to faithful men who will be able to teach others also" (2 Tim 2:2).

They Witness to the Truth to Those Outside the Church

Finally, our creeds and confessions serve us by defining the gospel of salvation for a fallen world as well as the eternal punishment to be suffered by those who reject it. Jesus called the church "the light of the world" (Matt. 5:14). Yet, we can only function as light if we continue in the truth.

We live in an age in which many groups claiming to be churches darken and pervert the truths of the Bible. This has compromised the uncompromising and urgent message of Scripture. When an unbeliever asks the church, "What do you believe," it is not enough to say, "We believe the Bible." In order to be a faithful and effective witness in a time of shifting doctrinal tides, we must say, "We have written out exactly what we believe the Bible teaches."

REFLECTION QUESTIONS

With what aspect(s) of having creeds and confessions do you struggle?

In what way(s) will creeds and confessions benefit you?

Conclusion

In conclusion, we reiterate that we are a confessional church because to be so means that we are a biblical church. God's holy Word is the foundation of our beliefs. The Word of God tests all that a Reformed Church believes and does.

As well, we are a confessional church because this unites us to the transcendent reality that there has always been a church and it has always believed certain essential teachings. As members of a confessional church, we are members of the one, true catholic, universal church across all times and all places.

Our prayer is that you too will see the great creeds and confessions of the ancient Church and Protestant Reformation as lost treasures desperately needed in today's world, and by you. We need their unchanging and uncompromising guidance and wisdom as we seek to be a light to the nations, always holding forth the word of life (Phil 2:16; NASB). May we join together in standing with the faith of our fathers in confessing the truth and humbling our pride to these great summaries of the Christian Faith.

2

The Attributes of God

Religion, the fear of God, must therefore be the element which inspires and animates all theological investigation. That must be the pulsebeat of the science. A theologian is a person who makes bold to speak about God because he speaks out of God and through God. To profess theology is to do holy work. It is a priestly ministration in the house of the Lord. It is itself a service of worship, a consecration of mind and heart to the honour of His name
(Herman Bavinck)

Reflection Question

Who is the God you worship? Describe him.

Thrilling Theology

WE ARE about to embark upon "holy work," as Dr. Bavinck said so eloquently in the above quotation. Theology is simply the study of God. As Christians, God himself calls us to know him with our minds so that we might know him experientially with our hearts. Thus, Jesus says the greatest commandment is to love God with our hearts *and* minds (Matt 22:37).

As we do so, recognize that theology is not just something that experts do. Instead of being an intellectual enterprise, theology is learning about the drama of God's Word and how I fit into that drama. The drama of the Bible is that God has performed amazing deeds and we participate in them. In her oft quoted words, Dorothy Sayers says this about Christian doctrine:

> Official Christianity, of late years, has been having what is known as bad press. We are constantly assured that the churches are empty because preachers insist too much upon doctrine—dull dogma as people call it. The fact is the precise opposite. It is the neglect of dogma that makes for dullness. The Christian faith is the most exciting drama that ever staggered the imagination of man—and the dogma is the drama.[1]

Dogma is what we confess to believe as Christians. As Sayers says, our beliefs are a thrilling story of creation, fall, redemption, and consummation. She goes on to speak of how God became a man in Jesus Christ, saying,

> Now, we may call that doctrine exhilarating, or we may call it devastating; we may call it revelation, or we may call it rubbish; but if we call it dull, then words have no meaning at all.[2]

The words we profess in "the good confession" are exhilarating, revealed words of God himself, and thus learning and loving them cannot be dull. This is why Sayers, in another essay, describes telling unbelievers the story of Christianity, of whom she says, ". . . they simply cannot believe that anything so interesting, so exciting, and so dramatic can be the orthodox creed of the Church."[3]

As we study our theology, keep in mind the masterful way in which God has orchestrated history as a drama in which he displays his handiwork in creation and mercy in redemption—for Christ came to place you into that drama.

The Attributes of God

The drama begins "in the beginning" with the God who created time and space as the stage upon which he would perform his drama, as the canvas upon which he would produce his masterpiece. We begin with

---

[1] Dorothy Sayers, "The Greatest Drama Ever Staged," in *The Whimsical Christian* (New York: Macmillan Publishing Co., Inc., 1978), 11.
[2] *Ibid.*, 15.
[3] Sayers, "The Dogma Is the Drama," in *The Whimsical Christian* (New York: Macmillan Publishing Co., Inc., 1978), 24.

God himself, the origin and substance of Christian theology. In beginning any discussion of Christian belief, we must begin with God. What is the God that we Christians talk about so much like? This is the question of his nature and attributes, to which we will now seek an answer. We turn to the *Belgic Confession of Faith*, article 1, as a summary of who God is. This article is entitled "Of the Nature of God," and says,

> We all believe with the heart and confess with the mouth that there is one only simple and spiritual Being, which we call God; and that He is eternal, incomprehensible, invisible, immutable, infinite, almighty, perfectly wise, just, good, and the overflowing fountain of all good.

Study Questions

Why do Scripture (Gen 1) and the *Belgic Confession* (art. 1) both begin with God, and not with man?

What do we mean when we speak of the "attributes" of God?

Explain the following attributes of God from article 1 of the *Confession* in your own words:

One
(Deut 6:4; Ps 115:3–8)

Simple
(Rom 3:26; 1 John 1:9)

The Good Confession

Spiritual
(John 4:24)

Eternal
(Pss 90:2, 102:27)

Incomprehensible
(Rom 11:33)

Invisible
(1 Tim 6:15–16)

Immutable
(Mal 3:6, Ps 102:25–27, Jas 1:17)

Infinite
(1 Kgs 8:27)

Almighty
(Gen 17:1, Isa 40:15, 17, 23; Rev 1:8)

The Attributes of God

Perfectly wise
(1 Tim 1:17; Rom 16:27)

Just
(Rom 3:25–26, 9:14)

Good
(Ps 136)

In what ways is the God of article 1 similar or different from the gods of other religions?

For Further Study

On article 1 of the *Belgic Confession* see Daniel Hyde, "We Confess: Article 1 (Part 1)." *The Outlook* Vol. 53, No. 4 (2003): 13–14 and "We Confess: Article 1 (Part 2). *The Outlook* Vol. 53, No. 5 (2003): 9–11.[4]

---

[4] For more information about *The Outlook* go online to www.reformedfellowship.net.

3

Knowing God in His Word

REFLECTION QUESTION

What does it mean to "know" God?
How does a person come to know God?

Knowing God

AT THIS point it behooves us to ask, "But how do we know that this is what God is like and even more, how can we even know God?" One of the foundational truths of the Christian Faith is that this invisible, infinite, eternal God has made himself known. We can know God! What a stupendous statement that is. Finite, temporal, mutable, and sinful human beings can know the God of whom we have just spoke. "But how?" A brief answer is in article 2 of our *Confession*, "Of the Knowledge of God":

> We know Him by two means: First, by the creation, preservation, and government of the universe; which is before our eyes as a most elegant book, wherein all creatures, great and small, are as so many characters leading us to *see clearly the invisible things of God*, even *his everlasting power and divinity*, as the apostle Paul says (Rom 1:20). All which things are sufficient to convince men and leave them without excuse. Second, He makes Himself more clearly and fully known to us by His holy and divine Word, that is to say, as far as is necessary for us to know in this life, to His glory and our salvation.

The Good Confession

God has revealed himself in two ways. The *Confession* uses the language of Psalm 19, which speaks of these two ways as two "books," creation and Scripture.

Study Questions

Article 2 speaks about the "revelation" of God in the creation and the Word of God. What is "revelation?" What does it mean to "reveal" something?

In speaking of the revelation of God in the "creation, preservation, and government of the universe," we call this the "general" revelation of God. Why?

The *Confession* speaks about what we can learn about God from the "book" of general revelation, echoing Psalm 19:1–6 and Romans 1:18–25. According to these texts, what can we learn of God from creation?

Is the knowledge of God in the book of creation sufficient for a sinner's salvation? Why or why not? (see below)

Canons of Dort, III/IV, 4

> There remain, however, in man since the fall, the glimmerings of natural light, whereby he retains some knowledge of God, and natural things, and of the difference between good and evil, and shows some regard for virtue and for good outward behavior. But so far is this light of nature from being sufficient to bring him to a saving knowledge of God and to true conversion that he is incapable of using it aright even in things natural and civil . . .

In the books of Holy Scripture, this God who is generally known as Creator in his creation has made himself "more clearly and fully known." Thus, we call this aspect of God's revelation "special revelation." What does this mean?

What is the purpose of God giving us the Bible?
(Deut 4:32–34; Ps 147:19–20; *Heidelberg Catechism* 19; *Canons of Dort* III/IV, 6)

What do we learn of God in special revelation?

An Inspired Word

We confess that God is "more clearly and fully known" to us in his Word. Our *Confession* now spends its next five articles exploring and explaining the Word in which God is most fully known. As historic Protestant Christians, we believe that in all our theology we must begin with God as he has revealed himself in his Word since we believe that the Scriptures alone are our only rule for doctrine (*sola Scriptura*). What is this Word like? What are its attributes and characteristics? We turn to article 3, "Of Holy Scripture":

> We confess that this Word of God was not sent nor delivered by the will of man, but that *men spake from God, being moved by the Holy Spirit*, as the apostle Peter says; and that afterwards God, from a special care which He has for us and our salvation, commanded His servants, the prophets and apostles, to commit His revealed word to writing; and He Himself wrote with His own finger the two tables of the law. Therefore we call such writings holy and divine Scriptures.

The Word of God is holy and sacred, which means that it is inspired. From this confession everything else that we have to say about the Word flows. Whatever we believe about the nature of Scripture will direct our thoughts about that Word. As you see above, article 3 has two parts: the giving of the Word of God by God and the writing of the Word of God by men. Because God gave the Word, what the prophets and apostles wrote down is the holy Word of God; therefore, it is without error and a sufficient rule for faith and life. If it is was not given by God or if only parts of it were, then it contains error and is insufficient and incomplete for our thoughts about God and how we live before his face (Latin, *coram Deo*).

Reflection Question

What does it say about God that he reveals himself to us sinful creatures in human words we can understand?

Study Questions

Look up the word "inspire/inspiration" in a dictionary. What is the definition?

Knowing God in His Word

What does the term "inspiration" mean when spoken of the Bible? (2 Tim 3:14–17) Is there a difference between the Scriptures' inspiration and Shakespeare causing us to say he was inspired when he wrote *Romeo & Juliet*?[1]

There are basically three ways of understanding the "inspiration" of Scripture:

1. Dictation: the emphasis is on God, who literally spoke/dictated his Word to the prophets and apostles.

2. Dynamic: the emphasis is on the men who wrote, as they put their religious thoughts down on paper.

3. Organic: emphasizes that the Word is both divine and human.

In light of these three descriptions above, where do 2 Timothy 3:16 and 2 Peter 1:20–21 fit? What do they say about *how* the prophets and apostles wrote the Word?

How much of the Bible is "inspired?"
(Matt 5:17; 1 Tim 3:16)

Why has God given us the Scriptures?

---

[1] The various translations of 2 Timothy 3:16 say:
"... *All Scripture is God–breathed* ..." *(NIV)*
"... *All Scripture is breathed out by God* ..." *(ESV)*
"... *All Scripture is inspired by God* ..." *(NASB)*
"... *All Scripture is given by inspiration of God* ..." *(NKJV)*

A Canonical Word

So we believe that God has spoken his inspired Word "to our fathers by the prophets" and "to us by his Son" (Heb 1:1), but the question is where? Which books can I read to hear his Word? This is the next logical question that we must ask ourselves. This is the question of the "canon" of holy Scripture to which article 4 directs our attention, which is entitled, "Of the Canonical Books of the Old and New Testaments":

> We believe that the Holy Scriptures are contained in two books, namely, the Old and New Testament, which are canonical, against which nothing can be alleged. These are thus named in the Church of God.
>
> The books of the Old Testament are the five books of Moses, to wit: Genesis, Exodus, Leviticus, Numbers, Deuteronomy; the book of Joshua, Judges, Ruth, the two books of Samuel, the two of the Kings, two books of the Chronicles, commonly called Paralipomenon, the first of Ezra, Nehemiah, Esther; Job, the Psalms of David, the three books of Solomon, namely, the Proverbs, Ecclesiastes, and the Song of Songs; the four great prophets, Isaiah, Jeremiah[2], Ezekiel, and Daniel; and the twelve lesser prophets, namely, Hosea, Joel, Amos, Obadiah, Jonah, Micah, Nahum, Habakkuk, Zephaniah, Haggai, Zechariah, Malachi.
>
> Those of the New Testament are the four evangelists, to wit: Matthew, Mark, Luke, and John; the Acts of the Apostles; the fourteen epistles of the apostle Paul, namely, one to the Romans, two to the Corinthians, one to the Galatians, one to the Ephesians, one to the Philippians, one to the Colossians, two to the Thessalonians, two to Timothy, one to Titus, one to Philemon, and one to the Hebrews; the seven epistles of the other apostles, namely, one of James, two of Peter, three of John, one of Jude; and the Revelation of the apostle John.

As Protestant Christians, we confess that God's Word is found in the sixty-six books (thirty-nine in the Old Testament and twenty-seven in the New Testament) that we call the Bible. These, and these only, are the holy, sacred, and inspired Word of God for the world to read and hear.

---

[2] I hope you have noticed that the book of Lamentations is not included in this list. The reason is that the Reformers often spoke of "Jeremiah" as a shorthand way of saying both books he wrote, the prophecy of Jeremiah and his Lamentations.

Knowing God in His Word

Reflection Question

How do we reconcile a belief in a fixed body of books as the Word of God in a relativistic culture, which says each culture creates its own "canon" of truth?

Study Questions

Look up the word "canon" (Greek, *kanōn*) in a dictionary (you may have to consult a theological dictionary). It is used in the New Testament in two senses: first, it is used to describe an ethical/theological "rule" (Gal 6:12–16), and, second, it is used to describe a geographically "bounded" area in which Paul had influence (2 Cor 10:13–16).

So, what does it mean when we use it in relation to Scripture?

Can we add to the "canon" of the Old and New Testaments? Why or why not? (Deut 12:32; Rev 22:18–19)

Is the canon of Scripture, therefore, "open" or "closed?" Do newly inspired words of God from prophets and apostles exist today? Why or why not?

Below (table 1) is a list of the Old and New Testament books, divided into traditional categories. If you do not already know the names of the books of Scripture, work on memorizing them (for a good challenge,

Jewish Old Testament	Christian Old Testament	New Testament
Law	*Law*	*Gospels*
Genesis	Genesis	Matthew
Exodus	Exodus	Mark
Leviticus	Leviticus	Luke
Numbers	Numbers	John
Deuteronomy	Deuteronomy	
		History
Prophets—Former	*Historical Books*	Acts
Joshua	Joshua	
Judges	Judges	*Epistles*
1/2 Samuel	Ruth	Romans
1/2 Kings	1/2 Samuel	1/2 Corinthians
	1/2 Kings	Galatians
Prophets—Latter	1/2 Chronicles	Ephesians
Major	Ezra	Philippians
Isaiah	Nehemiah	Colossians
Jeremiah	Esther	1/2 Thessalonians
Ezekiel		1/2 Timothy
	Wisdom	Titus
Minor	Job	Philemon
Hosea	Psalms	Hebrews
Joel	Proverbs	James
Amos	Ecclesiastes	1/2 Peter
Obadiah	Song of Songs	1/2/3 John
Jonah		Jude
Micah	*Prophets*	
Nahum	Major	*Apocalypse*
Habakkuk	Isaiah	Revelation
Zephaniah	Jeremiah	
Haggai	Lamentations	
Zechariah	Ezekiel	
Malachi	Daniel	
Writings	Minor	
Psalms	Hosea	
Job	Joel	
Proverbs	Amos	
Ruth	Obadiah	
Song of Songs	Jonah	
Ecclesiastes	Micah	
Lamentations	Nahum	
Esther	Habakkuk	
Daniel	Zephaniah	
Ezra	Haggai	
Nehemiah	Zechariah	
1/2 Chronicles	Malachi	

memorize both the Jewish and Christian order of the Old Testament books!).

An Authoritative Word

God has spoken, as article 3 declared, and we believe he is still speaking to his Church in the canonical books of Scripture, as article 4 declared. Because of this, these books alone are our source and foundation of theology and practice, doctrine and life. Yet, this begs an enormous question, "*How* do we know that *these* books are the inspired and canonical word of God?" Article 5 discusses the topic "Of the Authority of Holy Scripture," that is, how we know that these sixty-six books are the authoritative Word of God, saying,

> We receive all these books, and these only, as holy and canonical, for the regulation, foundation, and confirmation of our faith; believing without any doubt all things contained in them, not so much because the Church receives and approves them as such, but more especially because the Holy Spirit witnesses in our hearts that they are from God, and also because they carry the evidence thereof in themselves. For the very blind are able to perceive that the things foretold in them are being fulfilled.

Study Questions

What does it mean to receive the canonical books for the "regulation, foundation, and confirmation of our faith?"

What is the reason Protestants do not receive these books because of the Church's approval, as Rome says?
(Eph 2:19–20)

What are the two ways the *Confession* gives and which we as Protestants traditionally give as the reason why we know that our sixty-six books are the canon?

1.   (see 1 John 4:1–6, 5:6–13)

2.   (see Isa 7:14; Matt 1:23)

If one of the reasons we believe the canon to be God's Word is the witness of the Holy Spirit in our hearts, then cannot anyone claim a different Bible for the same reason?

A Sufficient Word

Because of all that we have said about the Word of God in articles 3–6, we conclude this section of our study by confessing to the world that Scripture alone is sufficient for the Church's theology, worship, and life. No man, church council, or *Confession of Faith*, for that matter, takes the place of the Holy Scriptures.

Since God has spoken, his Word is all we need. Because we have in his Word all we need, we reject everything that seeks to add to or subtract from this Word, even if it were an angel of heaven. Article 7 of the *Belgic Confession*, "Of the Perfection of Holy Scripture," states this in these words:

> We believe that those Holy Scriptures fully contain the will of God, and that whatsoever man ought to believe unto salvation is sufficiently taught therein. For since the whole manner of worship which God requires of us is written in them at large, it is unlawful for any one, though an apostle, to teach otherwise than we are now taught in the Holy Scriptures; *nay, though it were an angel from heaven*, as the apostle Paul says. For since it is forbidden to *add unto or take away anything from the Word of God*, it does thereby evidently appear that the doctrine thereof is most perfect and complete in all respects.
>
> Neither may we consider any writings of men, however holy these men may have been, of equal value with those divine Scriptures, nor ought we to consider custom, or the great multitude, or antiquity, or succession of times and persons, or

councils, decrees or statutes, as of equal value with the truth of God, since the truth is above all: *for all men are of themselves liars, and more vain than vanity itself.* Therefore we reject with all our hearts whatsoever does not agree with this infallible rule, as the apostles have taught us, saying, *Prove the spirits, whether they are of God.* Likewise: *If any one cometh unto you, and bringeth not this teaching, receive him not into your house.*

Reflection Question

If God has given us His Word, and that Word is found in the sixty-six books of the canon, *then* what does that say about other so-called books, teachers, miracles, signs and wonders?

Study Questions

What do we mean when we say that the Scriptures are "sufficient?"

Is Scripture "sufficient" for everything? If not, in which areas is it insufficient? (1 Pet 1:10–12)

What implications arise from saying Scripture is sufficient for worshipping God?

For Further Study

On article 2 of the *Belgic Confession* see Daniel Hyde, "We Confess: Article 2 (Part 1)." *The Outlook* Vol. 53, No. 6 (2003): 15–16 and "We Confess: Article 2 (Part 2)." *The Outlook* Vol. 53, No. 7 (2003): 9–10.

On article 3 of the *Belgic Confession* see Daniel Hyde, "We Confess: Article 3." *The Outlook* 53:8 (October 2003): 14–17.

On articles 4–5 of the *Belgic Confession* see Daniel Hyde, "We Confess: Articles 4 and 5." *The Outlook* 53:9 (November 2003): 7–9.

On articles 6–7 of the *Belgic Confession* see Daniel Hyde, "We Confess: Articles 6 and 7." *The Outlook* 53:10 (December 2003): 5–7.

On the doctrine of inspiration see B.B. Warfield, *Revelation and Inspiration*, The Works of Benjamin B. Warfield: Vol. I (Grand Rapids: Baker, reprinted 2000) and E.J. Young, *Thy Word is Truth* (Edinburgh: Banner of Truth, reprinted 1997).

On the Protestant doctrine of "Scripture alone" see W. Robert Godfrey, "What Do We Mean By *Sola Scriptura?*," in *Sola Scriptura!* (Morgan: Soli Deo Gloria, 1995), 1–26.

For a history of the New Testament canon, see F.F. Bruce, *The Canon of Scripture* (Downers Grove: IVP, 1988) and Herman N. Ridderbos, *Redemptive History and the New Testament Scriptures*, trans. H. De Jongste, (2nd rev. ed.; Phillipsburg: P&R, 1988).

For Even Further Study

During the Reformation the doctrine of Scripture and which books were Scripture was one of the foundational reasons for the Reformation itself. Because we believe and confess the sixty-six books of the Old and New Testaments alone are inspired (art. 3), canonical (art. 4), and authoritative (art. 5), we therefore reject the "apocryphal" books as uninspired, non-canonical, and non-authoritative in matters of doctrine, although, they are not utterly devoid of any use by the Church. This is not a hot-button issue to most of us today, but its discussion has enduring value as to where we can go to find the Word of God and which kinds of books we need to look out for. Article 6, "Of the Difference between the Canonical and Apocryphal Books," says,

> We distinguish these sacred books from the apocryphal, viz: the third and fourth books of Esdras, the books of Tobit, Judith, Wisdom, Jesus Sirach, Baruch, the Appendix to the book of Esther, the Song of the Three Children in the Furnace, the

History of Susannah, of Bel and the Dragon, the Prayer of Manasseh, and the two books of the Maccabees. All of which the Church may read and take instruction from, so far as they agree with the canonical books; but they are far from having such power and efficacy that we may from their testimony confirm any point of faith or of the Christian religion; much less may they be used to detract from the authority of the other, that is, the sacred books.

A Brief History of the Apocrypha

In the period of the ancient church (*ca.* 100–500), the church fathers (those early apologists, pastors, and theologians) never received the apocryphal (from the Greek word, *apokruphos*, meaning, "hidden") books as inspired books to be included in the canon. One example of this comes from St. Athanasius, the great defender of the orthodox doctrine of the Trinity at the Council of Nicea. In the year 367 he wrote a letter, in which he distinguished between the Old and New Testaments as the canon from the apocryphal books, saying, "But the former, my brethren, are included in the Canon, the latter being [merely] read."

In contrast, the Roman Catholic Church decreed at the Council of Florence (1438–1455) that the apocryphal books were inspired and canonical. As well, at the Council of Trent (1545–1563), the Council, which dealt with teachings of the Protestant Reformation, Rome reaffirmed that the apocryphal books were a part of the canon. Even worse, the Council of Trent declared that anyone who rejected the apocrypha is *anathema*, that is, under the curse of God. In contrast to Rome, but in harmony with the ancient church, the Protestant Reformers rejected the apocryphal books as canonical, although, as article 6 of the *Confession* says, "the Church may read and take instruction from" them. One way in which Reformed Protestants showed this is illustrated in the Dutch Bible (*Staten Bijbel*), translated and approved at the Synod of Dort (1618–19), in which the apocrypha was placed *after* the New Testament, *in small print*, and with this disclaimer, " . . . because they are not canonical, they are not to be read publicly in the congregation."

The Good Confession

Reasons for Rejecting the Apocrypha

Besides not being testified to by the Holy Spirit nor having the self-authentication that the Holy Scriptures have, there are many other reasons why we reject the Apocrypha as a part of the canon:

1. Jesus and the Apostles do not quote from them in the New Testament.

2. They were never included in the Hebrew canon (Old Testament). The Jews, who were "entrusted with the oracles of God" (Rom 3:2), never accepted them as canonical.[3]

3. They contain numerous historical inaccuracies, such as the following:

    a. The book of *Judith* calls Nebuchadnezzar king of Nineveh, although Scripture and history call him the king of Babylon.

---

[3] In Julius Africanus' (A.D. 200–245) letter to Origen, he disputes the authenticity of the apocryphal book, *The History of Susanna*, saying, "I cannot understand how it escaped you that this part of the book is spurious. For, in sooth, this section, although apart from this it is elegantly written, is plainly a more modern forgery. There are many proofs of this . . . "
1. "When Susanna is condemned to die, the prophet is seized by the Spirit, and cries out that the sentence is unjust. Now, in the first place, it is always in some other way that Daniel prophesies—by visions, and dreams, and an angel appearing to him, never by prophetic inspiration."
2. Daniel "detects them in a way no less incredible, which not even Philistion the playwriter would have resorted to. For, not satisfied with rebuking them through the Spirit, he placed them apart, and asked them severally where they saw her committing adultery. And when the one said, 'Under a holm-tree' (*prinoi*), he answered that the angel would saw him asunder (*prisein*); and in a similar fashion menaced the other who said, 'Under a mastich-tree' (*schinoi*), with being rent asunder (*schisthenai*). Now, in Greek, it happens that 'holm-tree' and 'saw asunder,' and 'rend' and 'mastich-tree' sound alike; but in Hebrew they are quite distinct."
3. His "more fatal objection" is "that this section, along with the other two at the end of it, is not contained in the Daniel received among the Jews. And add that, among all the many prophets who had been before, there is no one who has quoted from another word for word. For they had no need to go a-begging for words, since their own were true; but this one, in rebuking one of those men, quotes the words of the Lord: "The innocent and righteous shall thou not slay." From all this I infer that this section is a later addition. Moreover, the style is different."

b. The book of *Wisdom* attributes the Olympics to the days of Solomon (reigned 970–930 B.C.), although they did not exist until the days Greek Empire.

4. They contain fanciful stories, such as the following:

   a. In the book, *Bel and the Dragon*, Daniel proves to the king that his god is really no god at all, only a fierce dragon. He proves this by showing that the king's god does not eat the daily food offerings laid before his idol statue, but a dragon does, by laying out indigestible cake, which kills the dragon. As a result, Daniel is thrown into the lions' den.

   b. In the book of *Tobit*, Raphael the angel gives magical directions for driving away the devil by taking a fish's liver, burning it, and causing a magical smoke (6:6)

5. They contain false doctrines, such as the following:

   The book of *Tobit* says Raphael the angel accepted prayers offered to him (12:12), which angels never accept in Scripture (Rev 22:8–9)

4

The Holy Trinity

REFLECTION QUESTION

Why do Christians make such a big deal about the Trinity?
How important is the doctrine of the Trinity
for you and your salvation?

God's Triune Nature

Now that we have sufficiently explained what we believe about God's Word, we return to our exploration of who God is. Recall that in article 1 the *Confession* described God's nature and attributes. Yet, one thing we did not say about him makes us Christians. That one thing is the greatest, most mysterious of all biblical doctrines: the Holy Trinity. Here is the doctrine that distinguishes us from all other religions, faith systems, and philosophies in the world, a doctrine that is theologically precise and intellectually satisfying and mysterious. Article 8 is entitled "Of the Holy Trinity of Persons in One Divine Essence," and says,

> According to this truth and this Word of God, we believe in one only God, who is the one single essence, in which are three persons, really, truly, and eternally distinct according to their incommunicable properties; namely, the Father, and the Son, and the Holy Spirit. The Father is the cause, origin, and beginning of all things visible and invisible; the Son is the word, wisdom, and image of the Father; the Holy Spirit is the eternal power and might, proceeding from the Father and the Son. Nevertheless,

God is not by this distinction divided into three, since the Holy Scriptures teach us that the Father, and the Son, and the Holy Spirit have each His personality, distinguished by Their properties; but in such wise that these three persons are but one only God.

Hence, then, it is evident that the Father is not the Son, nor the Son the Father, and likewise the Holy Spirit is neither the Father nor the Son. Nevertheless, these persons thus distinguished are not divided, nor intermixed; for the Father has not assumed the flesh, nor has the Holy Spirit, but the Son only. The Father has never been without His Son, or without His Holy Spirit. For They are all three co-eternal and co-essential. There is neither first nor last; for They are all three one, in truth, in power, in goodness, and in mercy.

Did you recognize any of the language and terminology in article 8? If you have read any of the Church's creeds you will recognize that this article is based on the explanation of the Holy Trinity in the *Athanasian Creed*:

Athanasian Creed, lines 1–28

1. Whosoever will be saved, before all things it is necessary that he hold the catholic faith;
2. Which faith except every one do keep whole and undefiled, without doubt he shall perish everlastingly.
3. And the catholic faith is this: That we worship one God in Trinity, and Trinity in Unity;
4. Neither confounding the persons, nor dividing the substance.
5. For there is one person of the Father, another of the Son, and another of the Holy Spirit.
6. But the Godhead of the Father, of the Son, and of the Holy Spirit is all one, the glory equal, the majesty co-eternal.
7. Such as the Father is, such is the Son, and such is the Holy Spirit.
8. The Father is uncreated, the Son is uncreated, and the Holy Spirit is uncreated.
9. The Father is incomprehensible, the Son is incomprehensible, and the Holy Spirit is incomprehensible.

The Holy Trinity

10. The Father is eternal, the Son is eternal, and the Holy Spirit is eternal.
11. And yet there are not three eternals, but one eternal.
12. As also there are not three uncreated nor three incomprehensibles, but one uncreated and one incomprehensible.
13. So likewise the Father is almighty, the Son is almighty, and the Holy Spirit is almighty;
14. And yet there are not three almighties, but one almighty.
15. So the Father is God, the Son is God, and the Holy Spirit is God;
16. And yet they are not three Gods, but one God.
17. So likewise the Father is Lord, the Son is Lord, and the Holy Spirit is Lord;
18. And yet they are not three Lords, but one Lord.
19. For like as we are compelled by the Christian verity to acknowledge every person by himself to be God and Lord;
20. So we are forbidden by the catholic religion to say: There are three Gods or three Lords.
21. The Father is made of none, neither created nor begotten.
22. The Son is of the Father alone; not made nor created, but begotten.
23. The Holy Spirit is of the Father and of the Son; neither made, nor created, nor begotten, but proceeding.
24. So there is one Father, not three Fathers; one Son, not three Sons; one Holy Spirit, not three Holy Spirits.
25. And in this Trinity none is before, or after another; none is greater, or less than another.
26. But the whole three persons are co-eternal, and co-equal.
27. So that in all things, as aforesaid, the Unity in Trinity and the Trinity in Unity is to be worshipped.
28. He therefore that will be saved must thus think of the Trinity.

Heidelberg Catechism, Q&A 25

Since there is but one Divine Being, why do you speak of three persons: Father, Son, and Holy Spirit?

Because God has so revealed Himself in His Word, that these three distinct persons are the one, true, eternal God.

Study Questions

What is a simple definition of the doctrine of the Trinity?

In our discussion of the attributes of God, we said God is "one." But what do we mean when we say that he exists in "three Persons?"

The Scriptures reveal that God is both three and one. This is not contradictory but a mystery. As one writer says, "To say that God is One and Three is a contradiction only if we say that he is both in the same way and at the same time (i.e., God is One in person and Three in person). That is not what Christianity teaches. Instead, it teaches that God is one in *essence* and three in *person*."[1]

What role does mystery play in the doctrine of the Trinity by reflecting on the following statement: ""A God whom we could understand exhaustively, and whose revelation of Himself confronted us with no mystery whatsoever, would be a God in man's image, and therefore an imaginary God, not the God of the Bible at all."[2]

Biblical Evidence for the Trinity

This doctrine is the Faith of the Church. Where do we find it in Scripture? The creeds are great, and we believe biblical, but what is their biblical basis. After all, we believe in *sola Scriptura*, right? Article 9, "Of

---

[1] Michael Horton, *We Believe: Recovering the Essentials of the Apostles' Creed* (Nashville: Word, 1998), 80.

[2] J. I. Packer, *Evangelism & the Sovereignty of God* (Downers Grove: IVP, 1961), 24.

the Scripture Testimony of the Holy Trinity," gives some of the biblical testimony to the definition of the Trinity used in article 9:

> All this we know as well from the testimonies of Holy Writ as from their operations, and chiefly by those we feel in ourselves. The testimonies of the Holy Scriptures that teach us to believe this Holy Trinity are written in many places of the Old Testament, which are not so necessary to enumerate as to choose them out with discretion and judgment.
>
> In Genesis, chap. 1:26, 27, God says: *Let us make man in our image, after our likeness*, etc. *And God created man in his own image, male and female created he them*. And Gen. 3:22, *Behold, the man is become as one of us*. From this saying, Let *us* make man in *our* image, it appears that there are more persons than one in the Godhead; and when He says, *God* created, He signifies the unity. It is true, He does not say how many persons there are, but that which appears to us somewhat obscure in the Old Testament is very plain in the New. For when our Lord was baptized in Jordan, the voice of the Father was heard, saying, *This is my beloved Son*; the Son was seen in the water, and the Holy Spirit appeared in the shape of a dove. This form is also instituted by Christ in the baptism of all believers: *Make disciples of all the nations, baptizing them into the name of the Father and of the Son and of the Holy Spirit*. In the Gospel of Luke the angel Gabriel thus addressed Mary, the mother of our Lord: *The Holy Spirit shall come upon thee, and the power of the Most High shall overshadow thee; wherefore also the holt thing which is begotten shall be called the Son of God*. Likewise: *The grace of the Lord Jesus Christ, and the love of God, and the communion of the Holy Spirit, be with you all*. And [A.V.]: *There are three that bear record in heaven, the Father, the Word, and the Holy Ghost: and these three are one*.
>
> In all these places we are fully taught that there are three persons in one only divine essence. And although this doctrine far surpasses all human understanding, nevertheless we now believe it by means of the Word of God, but expect hereafter to enjoy the perfect knowledge and benefit thereof in heaven.
>
> Moreover, we must observe the particular offices and operations of these three persons towards us. The Father is called our Creator, by His power; the Son is our Savior and Redeemer, by His blood; the Holy Spirit is our Sanctifier, by His dwelling in our hearts.

This doctrine of the Holy Trinity has always been affirmed and maintained by the true Church since the time of the apostles to this very day against the Jews, Mohammedans, and some false Christians and heretics, as Marcion, Manes, Praxeas, Sabellius, Samosatenus, Arius, and such like, who have been justly condemned by the orthodox fathers. Therefore, in this point, we do willingly receive the three creeds, namely, that of the Apostles, of Nicea, and of Athanasius; likewise that which, conformable thereunto, is agreed upon by the ancient fathers.

This testimony to the Trinity is found in two places. Did you notice that? We find it in Scripture, our only source of doctrine, but also corroborated in Christian experience.

Reflection Question

How do mysterious doctrines like the Trinity affect our faith, worship, and Christian life?

Study Questions

What do the opening chapters of Genesis teach us about the Trinity? (Gen 1:1, 1:26–27, 3:22)

Does the Old Testament *clearly* teach the doctrine of the Trinity? (2 Cor 3:14–16) Defend your answer.

The Holy Trinity

What do the New Testament passages in *Belgic Confession*, article 9, teach us about the Trinity?

Can we *comprehend* the doctrine of the Trinity? Why or why not? (Rom 11:33–36)

According to Scripture, what is the role of God the Father? (Eph 1:3–6)

According to Scripture, what is the role of God the Son? (Eph 1:7–12)

According to Scripture, what is the role of God the Holy Spirit? (Eph 1:13–14)

The Deity of the Son

Since even the heretics believed that God the Father was God, we must examine who the Son of God and Holy Spirit are. This we do in articles 10–11. Here in article 10, "Of the Eternal Deity of the Son of God, our Lord Jesus Christ," we have impressed upon us that the Lord Jesus

Christ, whom we confessed God in articles 8–9, is the eternal Son of God.

> We believe that Jesus Christ according to His divine nature is the only begotten Son of God, begotten from eternity, not made, nor created (for then He would be a creature), but co-essential and co-eternal with the Father, *the very image of his substance and the effulgence of his glory*, equal unto Him in all things. He is the Son of God, not only from the time that He assumed our nature but from all eternity, as these testimonies, when compared together, teach us. Moses says that God created the world; and St. John says that all things were made by that Word which he calls God. The apostle says that God made the world by His Son; likewise, that God created all things by Jesus Christ. Therefore it must needs follow that He who is called God, the Word, the Son, and Jesus Christ, did exist at that time when all things were created by Him. Therefore the prophet Micah says: *His goings forth are from of old, from everlasting*. And the apostle: *He hath neither beginning of days nor end of life*. He therefore is that true, eternal, and almighty God whom we invoke, worship, and serve.

Reflection Question

What are the benefits to you as a believer in confessing the deity of Christ?

Study Questions

What does it mean that the Son of God is "begotten from eternity?" (Try wrapping your mind around that one! See John 8:58)

The Holy Trinity

According to John 1:1–5, who "created the heavens and the earth" in Genesis 1:1?

The Deity of the Holy Spirit

As with article 10, here in article 11 we will explore whom the Holy Spirit is in relation to the Father and the Son. Is the Spirit eternal? Is he God along with the Father and Son? This article, "Of the Person and Eternal Deity of the Holy Spirit," answers these questions, saying,

> We believe and confess also that the Holy Spirit from eternity proceeds from the Father and the Son; and therefore neither is made, created, nor begotten, but only proceeds from both; who in order is the third person of the Holy Trinity; of one and the same essence, majesty, and glory with the Father and the Son; and therefore is the true and eternal God, as the Holy Scriptures teach us.

Heidelberg Catechism, Q&A 53

> What do you believe concerning the "Holy Spirit?"
>
> First, that He is co-eternal God with the Father and the Son. Second, that He is also given unto me: by true faith makes me a partaker of Christ and all His benefits, comforts me, and shall abide with me forever.

REFLECTION QUESTION

What are the benefits to you as a believer in confessing the deity of the Holy Spirit?

Study Questions

In your own words, who is the Holy Spirit?

What does it mean that the Holy Spirit "from eternity proceeds?" Was the Holy Spirit created? (Heb 9:14)

As we study the identity of the Holy Spirit, we must keep in mind that there are two versions of the *Nicene Creed*, a Western and an Eastern version. The difference is only one word in Latin, *filioque*, which is translated, "and the Son." In the *Belgic Confession*, article 8 and 11, we as Protestants follow the Western Church's version of the *Nicene Creed*, which says,

> And we believe in the Holy Spirit, the Lord and Giver of life;
> who proceeds from the Father and the Son (Latin, *filioque*).

The doctrine of the Holy Spirit proceeding from the Father and the Son is called the "double procession" of the Holy Spirit. We believe it is a biblical doctrine, as the following questions and Scriptures show.

From whom does the Holy Spirit proceed according to John 14:16, 15:26; Rom 8:9; Gal 4:6?

From whom also does the Holy Spirit proceed according to John 15:26, 16:7; Rom 8:9; Gal 4:6?

The Holy Trinity

What do you think is the importance of saying that He "proceeds from the Father and the Son?"

For Further Study

On article 8 of the *Belgic Confession* see Daniel Hyde, "We Confess: Article 8." *The Outlook* 54:1 (January 2004): 11–14.

On article 9 of the *Belgic Confession* see Daniel Hyde, "We Confess: Article 9." *The Outlook* 54:1 (February 2004): 8–10.

On articles 10–11 of the *Belgic Confession* see Daniel Hyde, "We Confess: Articles 10–11." *The Outlook* 54:1 (March 2004): 11–13.

For Even Further Study

The *Belgic Confession* lists various religions and false teachers who rejected the Trinity. Look up each of the following in a theological and/or historical dictionary and write down what each taught/teaches about God?

Jews (Judaism)—

Mohammedans (Islam)—

Marcion—

Manes (or Mani; this was the founder of Manichaeism)—

Praxeas—

Sabellius—

Samosatenus (also known as Paul of Samosata)—

Arius—

5

Creation and Providence

Creation

As we conclude what we believe about God, recall what article 2 of the *Confession* taught. God is known by the two means of creation and the Word. We first dealt with the Word in articles 3–7 because it is the clear and sufficient revelation of God. Now we go back and look at what we believe creation and providence reveal about God in articles 12–13. We have explored the *nature* of God in his attributes and as a Triune God and now we explore the *works* of God in creation and providence. As Scripture declares and the creeds express, so too the *Belgic Confession* expresses that this Triune God has made "the heavens and the earth," all things "visible and invisible." He made the universe we see as well as the invisible world of angels and spirits we do not see. Article 12, "Of the Creation of the World, and of the Angels," says,

> We believe that the Father by the Word, that is, by His Son, has created of nothing the heaven, the earth, and all creatures, when it seemed good unto Him, giving unto every creature its being, shape, form, and several offices to serve its Creator; that He also upholds and governs them by His eternal providence and infinite power for the service of mankind, to the end that man may serve his God.
>
> He also created the angels good, to be His messengers and to serve His elect; some of whom are fallen from that excellency in which God created them into everlasting perdition, and the others have by the grace of God remained steadfast and continued in their first state. The devils and evil spirits are so depraved that they are enemies of God and every good thing; to the utmost of their power as murderers watching to ruin the Church and every member thereof, and by their wicked stratagems to destroy all;

and are, therefore, by their own wickedness adjudged to eternal damnation, daily expecting their horrible torments.

Therefore we reject and abhor the error of the Sadducees, who deny the existence of spirits and angels; and also that of the Manichees, who assert that the devils have their origin of themselves, and that they are wicked of their own nature, without having been corrupted.

Heidelberg Catechism, Q&A 26

What do you believe when you say: "I believe in God the Father Almighty, Maker of heaven and earth?"

That the eternal Father of our Lord Jesus Christ, who of nothing made heaven and earth with all that in them is, who likewise upholds, and governs the same by His eternal counsel and providence, is for the sake of Christ, His Son, my God and my Father, in whom I so trust as to have no doubt that He will provide me with all things necessary for body and soul; and further, that whatever evil He sends upon me in this troubled life, He will turn to my good; for He is able to do it, being Almighty God, and willing also, being a faithful Father.

Reflection Question

Instead of approaching the topic of creation from the point of view of when God created or how long it took God to create, begin by answering the question, "Why did God create?"

Study Questions

How did God create?

Creation and Providence

What does the Bible mean when it says
God created the "heavens?" (Gen 1:1)

What does the Bible mean when it says
God created the "earth?" (Gen 1:1)

What do "good angels" do?
What do evil angels (demons) do?

Providence

The drama of creation did not end once "God said . . . and it was so" (Gen 1:6–7). We must learn and experience that the same almighty God who created everything is also the Father who cares for everything. We call this care of God for his creation "providence." This providence extends to every atom, corner, and creature in the universe. Because he cares for us especially, we receive great practical benefit from knowing and experiencing this. Article 13 confesses "Of the Providence of God":

> We believe that the same good God, after He had created all things, did not forsake them or give them up to fortune or chance, but that He rules and governs them according to His holy will, so that nothing happens in this world without His appointment; nevertheless, God neither is the Author of nor can be charged with the sins which are committed. For His power and goodness are so great and incomprehensible that He ordains and executes His work in the most excellent and just manner,

even then when devils and wicked men act unjustly. And as to what He does surpassing human understanding, we will not curiously inquire farther than our capacity will admit of; but with the greatest humility and reverence adore the righteous judgments of God, which are hid from us, contenting ourselves that we are pupils of Christ, to learn only those things which He has revealed to us in His Word, without transgressing these limits.

This doctrine gives us unspeakable consolation, since we are taught thereby that nothing can befall us by chance, but by the direction of our most gracious and heavenly Father; who watches over us with a paternal care, keeping all creatures so under His power that *not a hair of our head (for they are all numbered), nor a sparrow can fall to the ground without the will of our Father*, in whom we do entirely trust; being persuaded that He so restrains the devil and all our enemies that without His will and permission they cannot hurt us.

And therefore we reject that damnable error of the Epicureans, who say that God regards nothing but leaves all things to chance.

Heidelberg Catechism, Q&A 27

What do you understand by the providence of God?

The almighty, everywhere-present power of God, whereby, as it were by His hand, He still upholds heaven and earth with all creatures, and so governs them that herbs and grass, rain and drought, fruitful and barren years, meat and drink, health and sickness, riches and poverty, indeed, all things come not by chance, but by His fatherly hand.

Heidelberg Catechism, Q&A 28

What does it profit us to know that God created, and by His providence upholds, all things?

That we may be patient in adversity, thankful in prosperity, and for what is future have good confidence in our faithful God and Father, that no creature shall separate us from His love, since all creatures are so in His hand, that without His will they cannot so much as move.

Creation and Providence

Reflection Question

How is God actively involved in your daily life?

Study Questions

What is "providence?" (Matt 6:25–34)
What is the opposite of providence?

How much does God control by his providence?
(Eph 1:11)

The following biblical texts show you how Scripture explains God's complete sovereignty and humanity's responsibility (notice, not "free will," which we will explain below). Read each biblical text then reflect upon the relationship between sovereignty and responsibility. Keep in mind the valuable concept of "antinomy," which is an *appearance* of contradiction between two facts.

> [10]when Rebecca had conceived children by one man, our forefather Isaac, [11]though they were not yet born and had done nothing either good or bad—in order that God's purpose of election might continue, not because of works but because of his call—[12]she was told, "The older will serve the younger." [13]As it is written, "Jacob I loved, but Esau I hated." (Rom 9:10–13)

The Good Confession

God's Sovereignty

Man's Responsibility

¹⁵See to it that no one fails to obtain the grace of God; that no "root of bitterness" springs up and causes trouble, and by it many become defiled; ¹⁶that no one is sexually immoral or unholy like Esau, who sold his birthright for a single meal. ¹⁷For you know that afterward, when he desired to inherit the blessing, he was rejected, for he found no chance to repent, though he sought it with tears. (Heb 12:15–17)

God's Sovereignty

Man's Responsibility

¹⁷For the Scripture says to Pharaoh, "For this very purpose I have raised you up, that I might show my power in you, and that my name might be proclaimed in all the earth." ¹⁸So then he has mercy on whomever he wills, and he hardens whomever he wills. (Rom 9:17–18)

God's Sovereignty

Man's Responsibility

²²For the Son of Man goes as it has been determined, but woe to that man by whom he is betrayed! (Luke 22:22)

God's Sovereignty

Man's Responsibility

¹⁶Brothers, the Scripture had to be fulfilled, which the Holy Spirit spoke beforehand by the mouth of David concerning Judas, who became a guide to those who arrested Jesus. ¹⁷For he was numbered among us and was allotted his share in this ministry. ¹⁸(Now this man bought a field with the reward of his wickedness . . .) ²⁰For it is written in the Book of Psalms,

Creation and Providence

"May his camp become desolate,
and let there be no one to dwell in it;"
and "Let another take his office."

[24]And they prayed and said, "You, Lord, who know the hearts of all, show which one of these two you have chosen [25]to take the place in this ministry and apostleship from which Judas turned aside to go to his own place." (Acts 1:16–18, 20, 24–25)

God's Sovereignty

Man's Responsibility

[22]Men of Israel, hear these words: Jesus of Nazareth, a man attested to you by God with mighty works and wonders and signs that God did through him in your midst, as you yourselves know—[23]this Jesus, delivered up according to the definite plan and foreknowledge of God, you crucified and killed by the hands of lawless men. (Acts 2:22–23)

If God's providence is over all, then is he
the author of sin and evil (see below)?

Nothing happens by chance, or without a very righteous decree of God (Eph 1:11; Matt 10:29; Prov 16:4). Nevertheless, God is not the Author of, or culpable for, any evil which takes place. For His power and goodness are so incomprehensible, that even when, in order to do something, He makes use of the devil or wicked men, whom He then justly punishes, yet He does not fail to decree and to do well and righteously His holy work (Acts 2:23; 4:27; Rom 9:19–20).[1]

When thinking of questions such as this
what should our attitude be?

---

[1] Theodore Beza, *The Christian Faith*, trans. James Clark (East Sussex: Focus Christian Ministries Trust, 1992), 2.

For Further Study

On article 12 of the *Belgic Confession* see Daniel Hyde, "We Confess: Article 12." *The Outlook* 54:4 (April 2004): 8–10.

On article 13 of the *Belgic Confession* see Daniel Hyde, "We Confess: Article 13." *The Outlook* 54:5 (May 2004): 9–11.

Some excellent books on the subject of God's providence are Paul Helm, *The Providence of God* (Contours of Christian Theology; Downer's Grove: IVP, 1994); Thomas Watson, *All Things for Good* (Edinburgh: Banner of Truth, reprinted 1994); Jerome Zanchius, *The Doctrine of Absolute Predestination*, trans. Augustus M. Toplady (Grand Rapids: Baker, reprinted 1977.

For Even Further Study

Investigate whom the Sadducees and Manichees were and write down your findings. What is a modern-day teaching that echoes that of the Sadducees? (Hint: "The cosmos is all that is or ever was or ever will be."[2]) What is a modern-day teaching that echoes that of the Manichees?

---

[2] Carl Sagan, *Cosmos* (NY: Ballantine, 1980), 1.

6

The Creation and Fall of Humanity

OUR DOGMATIC story now moves from the doctrine of God to the doctrine of man (*anthropology*). Looking at things in this order, we are reminded that we cannot truly know ourselves unless we first know the God who has made us. As John Calvin said,

> Our wisdom, in so far as it ought to be deemed true and solid Wisdom, consists almost entirely of two parts: the knowledge of God and of ourselves . . . For, in the first place, no man can survey himself without forthwith [immediately] turning his thoughts towards the God in whom he lives and moves . . . On the other hand, it is evident that man never attains to a true self-knowledge until he have previously contemplated the face of God.[1]

As we discuss ourselves, we move from the panoramic statement of article 12 that God made "the heaven, the earth, and all creatures" to focus in upon God's creation of man—and his subsequent sin against his Creator. This episode of this drama concludes in tragedy as we move from the heights of glory to the depths of depravity.

REFLECTION QUESTION

Who is man in relation to God?

---

[1] John Calvin, *Institutes of the Christian Religion*, ed. John T. McNeill, trans., Ford Lewis Battles, The Library of Christian Classics, vol. 20 (Philadelphia: The Westminster Press, 1960), 1.1.1–2.

Our Creation & Fall

Here in article 14, "Of the Creation, Fall, and Corruption of Man," we confess that God made us, in Adam, at the height of glory in the image of God (Latin, *imago Dei*). As the image bearer of God, Adam was made to be in a covenant relationship with God. However, we already know the end of the story—Adam broke that original covenant and therefore brought separation between God and us. As a result, we have also lost any ability to restore that covenantal relationship.

> We believe that God created man out of the dust of the earth and made and formed him after His own image and likeness, good, righteous, and holy, capable in all things to will agreeably to the will of God. But *being in honor, he understood it not*, neither knew his excellency, but willfully subjected himself to sin and consequently to death and the curse, giving ear to the words of the devil. For the commandment of life, which he had received, he transgressed; and by sin separated himself from God, who was his true life; having corrupted his whole nature; whereby he made himself liable to corporal and spiritual death. And being thus become wicked, perverse, and corrupt in all his ways, he has lost all his excellent gifts which he had received from God, and retained only small remains thereof, which, however, are sufficient to leave man without excuse; for all the light which is in us is changed into darkness, as the Scriptures teaches us, saying: *The light shineth in the darkness, and the darkness apprehended it not*; where St. John calls men darkness.
>
> Therefore we reject all that is taught repugnant to this concerning the free will of man, since man is but a slave to sin, and *can receive nothing, except it have been given him from heaven*. For who may presume to boast that he of himself can do any good, since Christ says: *No man can come to me, except the Father that sent me draw him?* Who will glory in his own will, who understands that *the mind of the flesh is enmity against God?* Who can speak of his knowledge, since *the natural man receiveth not the things of the Spirit of God?* In short, who dares suggest any thought, since he knows that *we are not sufficient of ourselves to account anything as of ourselves, but that our sufficiency is of God?* And therefore what the apostle says ought justly to be held sure and firm, that *God worketh in us both to will and to work, for his good pleasure*. For there is no understanding nor will conformable to the divine understanding and will but what Christ has

The Creation and Fall of Humanity

wrought in man; which He teaches us, when He says: *Apart from me ye can do nothing.*

Heidelberg Catechism, Q&A 6

Did God create man thus, wicked and perverse?

No, but God created man good and after His own image, that is, in righteousness and true holiness, that he might rightly know God his Creator, heartily love Him, and live with Him in eternal blessedness, to praise and glorify Him.

Canons of Dort III/IV, 1

Man was originally formed after the image of God. His understanding was adorned with a true and saving knowledge of his Creator, and of spiritual things; his heart and will were upright, all his affections pure, and the whole man was holy. But, revolting from God by the instigation of the devil and by his own free will, he forfeited these excellent gifts; and in the place thereof became involved in blindness of mind, horrible darkness, vanity, and perverseness of judgment; became wicked, rebellious, and obstinate in heart and will, and impure in his affections.

STUDY QUESTIONS

How did God create man? (Gen 2:7)

In classic Reformed theology, we distinguish the image of God in two senses, a broader image and a narrower image. The broad image speaks of everything that makes us human such as being religious, rationality, living in community, etc. The narrow image is that which Adam had in relation to God: knowledge of God, holiness, and righteousness.

What, then, does it mean that God made man in his image?

The Good Confession

In light of the above, what did Adam lose because of the Fall? (*Canons of Dort* III/IV, 1)

What did Adam still have after the Fall? (*Canons of Dort* III/IV, 4, 16)

What does Ephesians 4:24 and Colossians 3:10 say about the image of God in Christians?

Covenant

Since article 14 describes the creation of Adam and his original position (and subsequent "fall"), this is a good time to discuss what the Bible says about God's "covenants" with humanity. So I will explain some concepts and ideas here first, and then ask a few questions. In this section, we will discuss what we call the "covenant of works." When we move into article 17 and the promise of salvation in Christ, we will discuss what we call the "covenant of grace."

A "covenant" is a *mutual agreement* having two parts. In the first part, God comes to his people with the stipulations of the covenant including blessings and curses; in the second, his people respond either in obedience or in disobedience.[2]

---

[2] Zacharius Ursinus' *Commentary on the Heidelberg Catechism*, trans. George Willard (1852; Phillipsburg: P&R, reprinted 1985), 97.

Reflection Question

Before reading on, answer the question, "Did God make a covenant with Adam in the Garden?" Look up Hosea 6:7 and Isaiah 24:5 and think about how those verses affects your answer.

Covenant of Works

Classic Reformed theology teaches that there are two over-arching covenants in human history: the covenant of works (cf. *Westminster Confession of Faith* 7.2) and the covenant of grace. The covenant of works corresponds to the Law and the covenant of grace corresponds to the Gospel. The covenant of works is an outworking of the Law principle, "Do this and live" (Luke 10:28) and "cursed is everyone who does not continue to do everything written in the book of the Law" (Gal 3:10).

Through his prophet Hosea, the LORD prosecuted unfaithful Israel, comparing her to Adam in the garden, "Like Adam, they have broken the covenant—they were unfaithful to me there" (Hos 6:7). The analogy is that just as Adam broke a legal covenant with God so did Israel. This "covenant of works" was the covenant that God made with Adam in the Garden before the Fall. God put Adam on probation, so to speak, as God gave him the command not to eat of the tree of the knowledge of good and evil (Gen 2:16–17). If he did eat, the threatened curse was death, and the implied promise for obedience, then, was blessed fellowship with God.

Reflection Question

Was Adam able to keep the Law of God in the Garden perfectly? (Do not look below!)

God created Adam good, sinless, just, without defect and able to keep this covenant by the exercise of his free will (*Heidelberg Catechism*, Q&A 6; *Belgic Confession*, article 14; *Canons of Dort* III/IV, 1). As *Heidelberg Catechism* question and answer 9 says,

> Does not God, then, do injustice to man by requiring of him in His Law that which he cannot perform?
>
> No, for God so made man that he could perform it; but man, through the instigation of the devil, by willful disobedience deprived himself and all his descendants of this power.

Because Adam broke this covenant, God imputed his sin to us, since he is our representative (i.e., federal) head. This is why the Puritans said, "In Adam's fall, sinned we all." Everyone is born under Adam and everyone who is outside of Christ remains only in Adam and under the curse entailed by the covenant of works. For this reason, God placed cherubim and a flaming sword on the East side of the garden to prevent Adam from returning to the Garden (Gen 3:21–24).

If Adam had passed the probation by not eating of the forbidden tree, he would have represented us in meriting eternal life. As the Second Adam, the *Belgic Confession* describes Jesus Christ several times as meriting our salvation (e.g., Art. 22, 23, 24, 35).[3] What we say about Adam has weighty implications for what we say about our Lord himself, chiefly because of the clear teaching of the New Testament, which says that death came through one man (Rom 5:12ff), and therefore in Adam all die (1 Cor 15:21). In Romans 5:12–21 and 1 Corinthians 15:20–49, the New Testament parallels the "first man," Adam, with the second Adam, "the last man," Christ, who fulfilled the covenant of works, which Adam broke. Just as Adam disobeyed and plunged his seed (humanity) into death, the Second Adam (Christ) obeyed, fulfilled the conditions, and earned for his seed (the elect) eternal life.

Just because Scripture does not use the words "covenant of works," does not mean the concept is not biblical. When we use terms such as this and "Trinity," for example, we do so because they communicate Scriptural truths.

---

[3] Cf. Ursinus, *Commentary on the Heidelberg Catechism*, 325.

The Creation and Fall of Humanity

STUDY QUESTIONS

What did Adam's sin bring upon man? (Gen 2:17; Eph 2:1;
Canons of Dort III/IV, 2)

What is sin? (1 John 3:4; see below)

Westminster Shorter Catechism, Q&A 14

What is sin?

Sin is any want of conformity unto, or transgression of, the law of God.

What do we believe about "free will?"
(*Canons of Dort* III/IV, 1, 3, 10, Rejection of Errors 3, 4, 9)
Why? Give Scriptures to prove your answer.

Are we, after the Fall, able to obey the Law of God
and do the will of God? Why or why not?

The Effects of Adam's Sin in Us

Article 14 leaves us to contemplate the depths of Adam's fall and depravity. How does his sin affect us? Here in article 15, "Of Original Sin," we confess that the tragedy of his fall did not merely affect him, but it results in our being born with the guilt and pollution of his sin. We call this the doctrine of original sin. This original sin causes us to be sinners by nature *and* by imitation:

> We believe that through the disobedience of Adam original sin is extended to all mankind; which is a corruption of the whole nature and a hereditary disease, wherewith even infants in their mother's womb are infected, and which produces in man all sorts of sin, being in him as a root thereof, and therefore is so vile and abominable in the sight of God that it is sufficient to condemn all mankind. Nor is it altogether abolished or wholly eradicated even by baptism; since sin always issues forth from this woeful source, as water from a fountain; notwithstanding it is not imputed to the children of God unto condemnation, but by his grace and mercy is forgiven them. Not that they should rest securely in sin, but that a sense of this corruption should make believers often to sigh, desiring to be delivered from this body of death.
>
> Wherefore we reject the error of the Pelagians, who assert that sin proceeds only from imitation.

Reflection Question

How "healthy" is it for us as Christians to contemplate our sin?

Study Questions

Why do we call Adam's sin, which is passed down to us, "original sin?"

The Creation and Fall of Humanity

How do the images of a tree root and a water fountain's source vividly portray what has happened to us because of Adam's sin?

Why does Adam's original sin cause us to be sinners? (Rom 5:12–21)

What does the statement, "It is a corruption of the entire nature of man," mean?

Are babies innocent when born? Why or why not? (Job 14:1–4; Ps 51:5; Eph 2:3)

How can we remove our original sin?

If God forgave our original sin, why do we still sin? (Rom 7)

For Further Study

On *Belgic Confession* articles 14–15 see Daniel Hyde, "We Confess: Article 14." *The Outlook* 54:6 (June 2004): 10–13 and Daniel Hyde, "We Confess: Article 15." *The* Outlook 54:8 (September 2004): 7–9.

On the topic of man's creation, see Michael Scott Horton, *Putting Amazing Back Into Grace* (Nashville: Thomas Nelson, 1991), 7–21.

On the topic of the image of God, see Anthony A. Hoekema, *Created in God's Image* (Grand Rapids: Eerdmans, 1986) and Philip Edgcumbe Hughes, *The True Image* (Grand Rapids: Eerdmans, 1989).

On the topic of the biblical evidence that God made a covenant with Adam in the Garden see B. B. Warfield, "Hosea VI.7: Adam or Man?" *Selected Shorter Writings of Benjamin B. Warfield: 2 Volumes*, ed. John E. Meeter (3rd printing; Phillipsburg: P&R, 1980), I:116-29.

On the topic of the covenant of works see S. M. Baugh, "Covenant Theology Illustrated: Romans 5 on the Federal Headship of Adam and Christ." *Modern Reformation* (July/August, 2000): 16–23; M. G. Kline, "Gospel Until the Law: Rom 5:13–14 and the Old Covenant." *Journal of the Evangelical Theological Society* 34 (1991): 433–46.

On the topic of the imputation of Adam's sin to us, see the classic work of John Murray, *The Imputation of Adam's Sin* (Philipsburg: P&R, 1959).

On the topic of Adam's "Fall," see Horton, *Putting Amazing Back Into Grace*, 22–39.

On the topic of who Pelagius was and what is the danger of what he taught see the *Canons of Dort* III/IV, 2 as well as R.C. Sproul, "The Pelagian Captivity of the Church." *Modern Reformation* (May/June 2001): 22–23, 26–29.

7

Election

Episode three of this amazing drama now begins. We have discussed the God who made us in articles 1–13 and our rebellious fall into sin in articles 14–15. Thankfully creation and the fall are not the end of the dramatic story that is unfolding before us from the Scriptures. The *Belgic Confession* now moves from creation and fall to redemption.

Who redeems us? This is the question answered in articles 16–19 as we confess the doctrine of Christ (*Christology*). He is God's remedy to rescue man from his fallen state. This part of the drama is so amazing as it chronicles the plan of God, which existed even before he created Adam in his image. The electing plan of God reveals both the mercy and justice of God in choosing to save some from this depth of depravity and by passing over the rest in their depravity (art. 16). This merciful God manifested this electing plan for the first time as he promised the Gospel to send a seed to crush the serpent (art. 17). This seed came in the Person of our Lord Jesus Christ, the eternal Son of God in the flesh (art. 18), who is both God and man, yet one Person (art. 19).

Reflection Question

Why does the word "election" have such a
negative connotation in our time?

Elect in Christ

Although article 16 describes God's electing love after it describes the Fall, this love of God was already in place even before Adam had fallen.

Therefore, the Lord, seeing man would fall from the covenant God had made with him, graciously determined to save some out of the fallen mass of sinful humanity, while he justly has passed over others and left them in their sins. Article 16 is entitled "Of Divine Predestination," and says,

> We believe that, all the posterity of Adam being thus fallen into perdition and ruin by the sin of our first parents, God then did manifest Himself such as He is; that is to say, merciful and just: merciful, since He delivers and preserves from this perdition all whom He in His eternal and unchangeable counsel of mere goodness has elected in Christ Jesus our Lord, without any respect to their works; just, in leaving others in the fall and perdition wherein they have involved themselves.

Study Questions

What is the significance of discussing the doctrine of election after discussing the Fall?

Before discussing the doctrine of predestination, what must we understand about ourselves? (see below)

Canons of Dort I, 1

> As all men have sinned in Adam, lie under the curse, and are deserving of eternal death, God would have done no injustice by leaving them all to perish and delivering them over to condemnation on account of sin, according to the words of the apostle: "that every mouth may be stopped, and all the world may be brought under the judgment of God" (Rom 3:19). And: "for all have sinned, and fall short of the glory of God" (Rom 3:23). And: "For the wages of sin is death" (Rom 6:23).

Election

What two attributes of God does predestination manifest? (Rom 9:18, 22–23)

1. (*Canons of Dort* I, 2)

2. (*Canons of Dort* I, 6, 15)

What is the ulitmate reason God shows his mercy to us in election? (Rom 8:29, 9:16; Eph 1:5; *Canons of Dort* I, 7, 9, 10)

God does not just predestine *that* we will be saved (the end) but also *how* we will be saved (the means).
What is the means he uses to bring his elect to faith? (see below)

Canons of Dort I, 3

And that men may be brought to believe, God mercifully sends the messengers of these most joyful tidings to whom He will and at what time He pleases; by whose ministry men are called to repentance and faith in Christ crucified. "How then shall they call on Him in whom they have not believed? And how shall they believe in Him of whom they have not heard? And how shall they hear without a preacher? And how shall they preach except they are sent?" (Rom 10:14–15).

How sure is God's electing grace? (*Canons of Dort* I, 7, 11)

How is God just in "leaving" or "passing by" those he
does not elect in mercy? Is this fair? (see below)

Canons of Dort I, 15

> What peculiarly tends to illustrate and recommend to us the eternal and unmerited grace of election is the express testimony of sacred Scripture that not all, but some only, are elected, while others are passed by in the eternal decree; whom God, out of His sovereign, most just, irreprehensible, and unchangeable good pleasure, has decreed to leave in the common misery into which they have willfully plunged themselves, and not to bestow upon them saving faith and the grace of conversion; but, permitting them in His just judgment to follow their own ways,[2] at last, for the declaration of His justice, to condemn and punish them forever, not only on account of their unbelief, but also for all their other sins. And this is the decree of reprobation, which by no means makes God the author of sin (the very thought of which is blasphemy), but declares Him to be an awful, irreprehensible, and righteous judge and avenger thereof.

How does knowing the sovereignty of God in election
benefit us? (Rom 11:33–36; *Canons of Dort* I, 12–13, 16, 18)

Should we believe, teach, and preach the doctrine of
predestination? If so, how? (see below)

Canons of Dort I,14

> As the doctrine of divine election by the most wise counsel of God was declared by the prophets, by Christ Himself, and by the apostles, and is clearly revealed in the Scriptures both of the Old and the New Testament, so it is still to be published in due time and place in the Church of God, for which it was peculiarly

designed, provided it be done with reverence, in the spirit of discretion and piety, for the glory of God's most holy Name, and for enlivening and comforting His people, without vainly attempting to investigate the secret ways of the Most High.

What do we believe about the children of believers who die in infancy? (see below)

Canons of Dort 1,17

Since we are to judge of the will of God from His Word, which testifies that the children of believers are holy, not by nature, but in virtue of the covenant of grace, in which they together with the parents are comprehended, godly parents ought not to doubt the election and salvation of their children whom it pleases God to call out of this life in their infancy.

Election & Evangelism

Let us say a brief word about why election and evangelism are *not* contradictory, mutually exclusive ideas. Election does not make us the "frozen chosen," but in fact, believing in the biblical doctrine of election is precisely the reason why we witness to Christ's resurrection and saving grace. He has chosen an innumerable number of men, women, and children (Rev 7:14) who need to hear the Gospel in order to be saved.

So how exactly do Reformed Christians evangelize? First, pray for the lost. Ask God to give you opportunities to speak of the Gospel. Ask God to open their hearts and ears to hear and heed the message.

Second, get to know your unsaved neighbors and cultivate a trusting relationship with them. When you speak with them, do so in love.

We have a theology of creation. This means that we can have real relationships with non-believers and really care about them.

Third, because "faith comes by hearing, and hearing by the word of Christ" (Rom 10:17), invite unbelievers to worship to hear the word preached. Help them through the worship. Open the Bible for them. Explain what is going on. And by all means, discuss what was preached after the service. A great quote on preaching in this light is from Dorothy Sayers, who said,

> Let us, in heaven's name, drag out the divine drama from under the dreadful accumulation of slipshod thinking and trashy sentiment heaped upon it, and set it on an open stage to startle the world into some sort of vigorous reaction. If the pious are the first to be shocked, so much the worse for the pious—others will enter the Kingdom of Heaven before them. If all men are offended because of Christ, let them be offended; but where is the sense of their being offended at something that is not Christ and is nothing like Him? We do Him singularly little honor by watering down till it could not offend a fly. Surely it is not the business of the Church to adapt Christ to men, but to adapt men to Christ.[1]

For Further Study

On *Belgic Confession* article 16 see Daniel Hyde, "We Confess: Article 16." *The Outlook* 54:9 (October 2004): 6–8.

On election and the practical benefits it causes in us, see Horton, *Putting Amazing Back Into Grace*, 40–74.

Three excellent books on Reformed evangelism are *Tell the Truth* by Will Metzger (Downers Grove: IVP, 2002), *God-Centered Evangelism* by R. B. Kuiper (Edinburgh: Banner of Truth, 1978), and J.I. Packer, *Evangelism and the Sovereignty of God* (Downers Grove: IVP, 1961).

---

[1] Sayers, "The Dogma Is the Drama," 27.

8

The Covenant of Grace

Reflection Question

How important in the life of the church, your family, and your individual spirituality are the promises of God?

The Promise of Christ

GOD LIFTED the curtain of his secret, eternal plan to save *from eternity* and executed that plan *in history*. The God who had already decided to save an innumerable multitude (Rev 7:9) now reveals that he would actually save this number by the means of his only-begotten Son, who would become our divine-human Savior. The *Confession* says this in article 17, "Of the Restoration of Natural Man through the Son of God":

> We believe that our most gracious God, in His admirable wisdom and goodness, seeing that man had thus thrown himself into physical and spiritual death and made himself wholly miserable, was pleased to seek and comfort him, when he trembling fled from His presence, promising him that He would give His Son (who would be *born of a woman*) *to bruise the head of the serpent* and to make him blessed.

STUDY QUESTIONS

Who had the "free will" after Adam's "Fall" in Genesis 3?

Why do we speak of Genesis 3:15 as the "mother promise?"

How did this promise unfold in the history of redemption? (see below)

Heidelberg Catechism, Q&A 19

From where do you know this?

From the Holy Gospel, which God Himself first revealed in Paradise, afterwards proclaimed by the holy patriarchs and prophets, and foreshadowed by the sacrifices and other ceremonies of the law, and finally fulfilled by His well-beloved Son.

Were the Old Testament saints saved by faith in Christ as we are? (see below)

"The Son is fully contained in the books of the Old Testament, so that the men of those times were saved by faith in Jesus Christ who was to come."[1]

Bentheim Confession, article 8

"Concerning the Efficacy of the Merit of Christ"

---

[1] Beza, *The Christian Faith*, 9.

Whether you believe that no salvation is able to be possessed and retained apart from Christ and therefore, the fathers of the Old Testament have been justified and saved no less by faith in Christ, at that time about to come, than we in the New Testament are justified and saved by faith in Christ now displayed.[2]

How does Galatians 4:4 show the fulfillment of Genesis 3:15?

The Covenant of Grace

We have already seen that in eternity, the Triune God had already made a mutual covenant between the members of the Trinity, to elect, redeem, and sanctify a people for their own glory. We call that the covenant of redemption. Then in time, space, and history, God made a covenant of works with Adam, and all humanity in him, before the Fall. Now we turn to the second of these covenants in time, space, and history, the covenant of grace.

You may be asking why this is so important to learn. It is because "Reformed" means more than just the so-called "Five Points of Calvinism." These five points are not the essence of what Reformed Churches teach and believe. That is partially our fault as Reformed churches, because we over-emphasize these doctrines, which really are only a very small part of who we are. To be Reformed, is to live in covenant with God. To think as Reformed Christians is to think covenantally. To worship as Reformed churches is to worship covenantally. To read the Bible, as Reformed Christians is to read it in a covenantal way, as it has one message—that God has come to the rescue of fallen man. This one message progressively unfolded through the Old Testament until its culmination in the New Testament. This is who we are as Reformed churches. One can hardly read the Bible without seeing how the term "covenant" shows up in page

---

[2] James T. Dennison, Jr., "The Bentheim Confession (1613/1617)." *Kerux: The Journal of the Northwest Theological Seminary* 20:2 (September 2005): 8–9.

after page. The Hebrew word for covenant, *berith*, is used 287 in the Old Testament alone,.

Article 17 mentions God's promise to send the "seed," Jesus Christ, to save his people. This is where we discuss the covenant of grace. The covenant of grace began with the "mother promise" of Genesis 3:15. It is one in essence throughout redemptive history, but varied in administration. It began in the Garden, after the Fall, continued with Noah, ratified with Abraham, and later Israel, and fulfilled in the New Covenant. It is the good news that God saves sinners by his undeserved favor (Eph 2:14–18); that this seed, Jesus Christ, has met the terms of the covenant of works for us so that we might live (Gal 2:15–21). Thus, when we say "covenant of grace" we mean nothing more than the Gospel.

The essence of the covenant of grace is "I will be your God, you will be my people" (Gen 17:7; Rev 21:3). This is a gracious promise to sinners fulfilled in the incarnation, obedience, suffering and death of Christ. In contrast with the covenant of works, God initiated the covenant of grace out of grace and mercy, with elect sinners, in Christ. He promises redemption (Gen 3:14–16; 15; 17:1–17), arranges an entire history of salvation full of types and shadows of redemption (Col 2:17; Heb 10:1) from Noah to Moses to David, which finds its final fulfillment in the incarnation, obedience, death and resurrection of his well-beloved Son, Jesus (Luke 3:22; Heb 9:14–28). The covenant of grace is gracious only for sinners to whom God grants saving faith. The covenant of grace, though quite different in principle, is similar in administration to the covenant of works in that it also has a condition. Whereas the condition of the covenant of works was, "do this and live," the condition of the covenant of grace is faith alone, in Christ the Savior alone, by which instrument one receives Christ's imputed righteousness. Scripture teaches that God graciously grants this condition of the covenant to his elect (Rom 3:19–5:21; Eph 2:8–10). The covenant of grace is monergistic, i.e., God initiates and fulfills it. It is gracious, i.e., it is marked not by, "Do this and live," but "since you have not done this, I will do it for you and you will live" (e.g., Jer 31; Rom 5:8).[3]

---

[3] This is the historic Reformed covenant theology taught by John Calvin, Caspar Olevianus, Zacharius Ursinus, Johannes Wollebius, Amandus Polanus, William Bucanus, Johannes Cocceius, Herman Witsius and more recently by Charles Hodge and Louis Berkhof. This is the view of the *Westminster Confession Faith* and the *Three Forms of Unity*.

The Covenant of Grace

STUDY QUESTIONS

What do you have to do to get into the covenant of grace? To stay in?

How is the covenant of grace similar/different than the covenant of works made with Adam in the Garden of Eden?

For Further Study

On *Belgic Confession* article 17 see Daniel Hyde, "We Confess: Article 17." *The Outlook* 54:10 (November 2004): 7–10.

9

Jesus Christ

Reflection Question

Why did God become man?

The Incarnation

THE PROMISE of the Son of God to be born of a woman is a marvelous mystery. How exactly could this be? Here in article 18, "Of the Incarnation of the Son of God," the answer to this question of how the Son would become our Savior is given. The eternal Son would become our Savior by becoming the Lord Jesus Christ. He would become our Savior by being incarnate by the power of the Holy Spirit in the womb of the Virgin Mary:

> We confess, therefore, that God has fulfilled the promise which He made to the fathers by the mouth of His holy prophets, when He sent into the world, at the time appointed by Him, His own only-begotten and eternal Son, who *took upon Him the form of a servant* and *became like unto man*, really assuming the true human nature with all its infirmities, sin excepted; being conceived in the womb of the blessed virgin Mary by the power of the Holy Spirit without the means of man; and did not only assume human nature as to the body, but also a true human soul, that He might be a real man. For since the soul was lost as well as the body, it was necessary that He should take both upon Him, to save both.
>
> Therefore we confess (in opposition to the heresy of the Anabaptists, who deny that Christ assumed human flesh of His mother) that Christ *partook of the flesh and blood of the children*;

that He is a *fruit of the loins of David after the flesh; born of the seed of David according to the flesh; a fruit of the womb of Mary; born of a woman; a branch of David; a shoot of the root of Jesse; sprung from the tribe of Judah;* descended from the Jews according to the flesh; of the seed of Abraham, since (A.V.) *he took on him the seed of Abraham,* and *was made like unto his brethren in all things, sin excepted;* so that in truth He is our IMMANUEL, that is to say, *God with us.*

Heidelberg Catechism, Q&A 35

What is the meaning of "conceived by the Holy Spirit, born of the virgin Mary?"

That the eternal Son of God, who is and continues true and eternal God, took upon Himself the very nature of man, of the flesh and blood of the virgin Mary, by the operation of the Holy Spirit; so that He might also be the true seed of David, like unto His brethren in all things, except for sin.

Heidelberg Catechism, Q&A 36

What benefit do you receive from the holy conception and birth of Christ?

That He is our Mediator, and with His innocence and perfect holiness covers, in the sight of God, my sin, wherein I was conceived.

This article of our *Confession* is divided into two parts: 1) the description of the incarnation, and, 2) the biblical testimony to the true humanity of Jesus Christ in opposition to the Anabaptist sects, who not only lived during the Reformation, but who also continue to plague the Church today.

Study Questions

Where in the Old Testament do we find the promise of the
coming of God in the flesh (the Incarnation)
"by the mouth of His holy prophets?"

Jesus Christ

If Jesus Christ was born of a sinful woman, how could he be born sinless? (Matt 1:18–20; Luke 1:34–35)

If man comprises a body and soul, and both are sinful, why was it necessary for Jesus Christ to have both?

The Two Natures of Christ

Now we come to one of the greatest questions of the Christian Faith. We have already confessed that Jesus Christ is the eternal Son of God (art. 10); but we also confessed him a true human being. How do these two natures, divine and human, relate to each other? We confess this great mystery with two thousand years of Christians.

Article 19 of the *Confession*, "Of the Hypostatic Union or of the Two Natures in the Person of Christ," is a summary and explanation of the balanced teaching of the ancient *Athanasian Creed* and *Definition of Chalcedon*:

> We believe that by this conception the person of the Son is inseparably united and connected with the human nature; so that there are not two Sons of God, nor two persons, but two natures united in one single person; yet each nature retains its own distinct properties. As, then, the divine nature has always remained uncreated, without beginning of days or end of life, filling heaven and earth, so also has the human nature has not lost its properties but remained a creature, having beginning of days, being a finite nature, and retaining all the properties of a real body. And though He has by His resurrection given immortality to the same, nevertheless He has not changed the reality of His human nature; forasmuch as our salvation and resurrection also depend on the reality of His body.
>
> But these two natures are so closely united in one person that they were not separated even by His death. Therefore that which He, when dying, commended into the hands of His Father, was a real human spirit, departing from His body. But in the meantime the divine nature always remained united with the human, even

when He lay in the grave; and the Godhead did not cease to be in Him, any more than it did when He was an infant, though it did not so clearly manifest itself for a while. Wherefore we confess that He is very God and very man: very God by His power to conquer death; and very man that He might die for us according to the infirmity of His flesh.

Heidelberg Catechism, Q&A 47

But is not Christ with us even unto the end of the world, as He has promised?

Christ is true man and true God. According to His human nature He is now not on earth, but according to His Godhead, majesty, grace, and Spirit, He is at no time absent from us.

Heidelberg Catechism, Q&A 48

But are not, in this way, the two natures in Christ separated from one another, if the manhood is not wherever the Godhead is?

Not at all, for since the Godhead is incomprehensible and everywhere present, it must follow that it is indeed beyond the bounds of the manhood which it has assumed, but is yet nonetheless in the same also, and remains personally united to it.

Reflection Question

Why do we spend so much time and so much effort to be precise on such doctrines as how the divine and human natures relate in the person of Christ?

As we study the "Person of Christ," that is, that he is one person with two natures, it is of the utmost importance to study the Scriptures with reverence and humility. This is one of the most profound and mysterious doctrines that we confess to believe. The great Reformer John Calvin said,

> It is very easy to see how beautifully they [Christ's two natures] accord with each other, provided they have a sober interpreter, one

who examines these great mysteries with the reverence which is meet.[1]

Also, as we study this amazing topic, let us keep in mind that this issue has been discussed, debated, and settled by the Fourth Ecumenical Council at Chalcedon in A.D. 451:

The Definition of Chalcedon (451)

> We, then, following the holy Fathers, all with one consent, teach men to confess one and the same Son, our Lord Jesus Christ, the same perfect in Godhead and also perfect in manhood; truly God and truly man, of a reasonable [rational] soul and body; consubstantial [coessential] with the Father according to the Godhead, and consubstantial with us according to the Manhood; in all things like unto us, without sin; begotten before all ages of the Father according to the Godhead, and in these latter days, for us and for our salvation, born of the Virgin Mary, the Mother of God according to the Manhood; one and the same Christ, Son, Lord, Only-begotten, to be acknowledged in two natures, inconfusedly, unchangeably, indivisibly, inseparably; the distinction of the natures being by no means taken away by the union, but rather the property of each nature being preserved, and concurring in one Person and Subsistence, not parted or divided into two persons, but one and the same Son, and only begotten, God the Word, the Lord Jesus Christ, as the prophets from the beginning [have declared] concerning him, and the Lord Jesus Christ himself has taught us, and the Creed of the holy Fathers has handed down to us.

Athanasian Creed, lines 29–44

> 29. Furthermore it is necessary to everlasting salvation that he also believe rightly the incarnation of our Lord Jesus Christ.
>
> 30. For the right faith is that we believe and confess that our Lord Jesus Christ, the Son of God, is God and man.
>
> 31. God of the substance of the Father, begotten before the worlds; and man of the substance of his mother, born in the world.

---

[1] John Calvin, *Institutes*, 2.14.4.

32. Perfect God and perfect man, of a reasonable soul and human flesh subsisting.
33. Equal to the Father as touching his Godhead, and inferior to the Father as touching his manhood.
34. Who, although He is God and man, yet He is not two, but one Christ.
35. One, not by conversion of the Godhead into flesh, but by taking of the manhood into God.
36. One altogether, not by confusion of substance, but by unity of person.
37. For as the reasonable soul and flesh is one man, so God and man is one Christ.
38. Who suffered for our salvation, descended into hell, rose again the third day from the dead;
39. He ascended into heaven, He sits at the right hand of the Father, God Almighty;
40. From there He shall come to judge the living and the dead.
41. At whose coming all men shall rise again with their bodies;
42. And shall give account of their own works.
43. And they that have done good shall go into life everlasting. And they that have done evil into everlasting fire.
44. This is the catholic faith, which except a man believe faithfully, he cannot be saved.

Study Questions

Describe the divine nature of Christ.

Jesus Christ

Describe the human nature of Christ.

Are the two natures of Christ in any way confused or changed by their union? Why or why not?

Are the two natures of Christ divided or separated by being distinct natures? Why or why not?

What benefit(s) do we receive from his divine nature?

What benefit(s) do we receive from his human nature?

For Further Study

On *Belgic Confession* articles 18 and 19 see Daniel Hyde, "We Confess: Article 18." *The Outlook* 54:11 (December 2004): 7–9 and Daniel Hyde, "We Confess: Article 19." *The Outlook* 55:1 (January 2005): 6–8.

On the Incarnation, see Horton, *Putting Amazing Back Into Grace*, 75–84.

10

The Death of Christ

Reflection Question

How are you, as a sinner, able to stand before a holy God?

Brief Explanation of Articles 20–26

IN ARTICLES 16–19, we confessed redemption particularly in terms of the Person of the Redeemer. In articles 20–26, we are still confessing the third part of our dogmatic drama, namely, redemption. The particular focus is on the cause (grace alone), ground (Christ alone), and instrument (faith alone) of our redemption. We call these things the doctrine of salvation (*soteriology*).

In this part of the drama, we learn that redemption from sin's guilt and pollution is a result of what Christ alone has done for us. As the head of the covenant of grace, Jesus Christ has won two great benefits for us: justification to deal with sin's guilt (arts. 20–23) and sanctification to deal with sin's pollution (arts. 24–26).

The Justice & Mercy of the Father

We begin this section by confessing what God the Father has done to fulfill his promise of a Savior, which we confessed in article 17. The heart of God as Father is revealed here as we confess him to have sent his eternal, only-begotten Son, to satisfy the justice of God while at the same time revealing the mercy of God. Our Savior Jesus Christ nullified the penalty of the broken covenant of works while he manifested his overflowing grace and mercy in the covenant of grace. This is expressed in article 20 of the *Belgic Confession*, "Of the Means of Redemption Through the Declaration of Justice and Mercy of God in Christ," which says,

> We believe that God, who is perfectly merciful and just, sent His Son to assume that nature in which the disobedience was committed, to make satisfaction in the same, and to bear the punishment of sin by His most bitter passion and death. God therefore manifested His justice against His Son when He laid our iniquities upon Him, and poured forth His mercy and goodness on us, who were guilty and worthy of damnation, out of mere and perfect love, giving His Son unto death for us, and raising Him for our justification, that through Him we might obtain immortality and life eternal.

Study Questions

Why did God's justice need to be "satisfied?"
(*Canons of Dort* II, 1–3; see below)

Heidelberg Catechism, Q&A 12

> Since, then, by the righteous judgment of God we deserve temporal and eternal punishment, how may we escape this punishment and be again received into favor?
>
> God wills that His justice be satisfied; therefore, we must make full satisfaction to that justice, either by ourselves or by another.

Heidelberg Catechism, Q&A 13

> Can we ourselves make this satisfaction?
>
> Certainly not; on the contrary, we daily increase our guilt.

Heidelberg Catechism, Q&A 14

> Can any mere creature make satisfaction for us?
>
> None; for first, God will not punish any other creature for the sin which man committed; and further, no mere creature can sustain the burden of God's eternal wrath against sin and redeem others from it.

Heidelberg Catechism, Q&A 15.

> What kind of mediator and redeemer, then, must we seek?

The Death of Christ

One who is a true and righteous man, and yet more powerful than all creatures, that is, one who is also true God.

Why do we need a human Savior? (see below)

Heidelberg Catechism, Q&A 16

> Why must He be a true and righteous man?
>
> Because the justice of God requires that the same human nature which has sinned should make satisfaction for sin; but one who is himself a sinner cannot satisfy for others.

Why do we need a Savior who is God? (see below)

Heidelberg Catechism, Q&A 17

> Why must He also be true God?
>
> That by the power of His Godhead He might bear in His manhood the burden of God's wrath, and so obtain for and restore to us righteousness and life.

Heidelberg Catechism, Q&A 18

> But who now is that Mediator, who in one person is true God and also a true and righteous man?
>
> Our Lord Jesus Christ, who is freely given unto us for complete redemption and righteousness.

The Good Confession

To whom was God just in the death of Christ?
To whom was he merciful?

What does it mean that the death of Christ is *sufficient*?
(see below)

Canons of Dort II, 3

> The death of the Son of God is the only and most perfect sacrifice and satisfaction for sin, and is of infinite worth and value, abundantly sufficient to expiate the sins of the whole world.

Canons of Dort II, 4

> This death is of such infinite value and dignity because the person who submitted to it was not only truly and perfectly a holy man, but also, the only begotten Son of God, of the same eternal and infinite essence with the Father and the Holy Spirit, which qualifications were necessary to constitute Him a Savior for us; and, moreover, because it was attended with a sense of the wrath and curse of God due to us for sin.

What does it mean that the death of Christ is *efficient*?
(see below)

Canons of Dort II, 8

> For this was the sovereign counsel and most gracious will and purpose of God the Father that the quickening and saving efficacy of the most precious death of His Son should extend to all the elect, for bestowing upon them alone the gift of justifying faith, thereby to bring them infallibly to salvation; that is, it was the will of God that Christ by the blood of the cross, whereby He confirmed the new covenant, should effectually redeem out of every people, tribe, nation, and language, all those, and those only, who were from

eternity chosen to salvation and given to Him by the Father; that He should confer upon them faith, which, together with all the other saving gifts of the Holy Spirit, He purchased for them by His death; should purge them from all sin, both original and actual, whether committed before or after believing; and having faithfully preserved them even to the end, should at last bring them, free from every spot and blemish, to the enjoyment of glory in His own presence forever.

Canons of Dort II, 9

This purpose, proceeding from everlasting love towards the elect, has from the beginning of the world to this day been powerfully accomplished, and will henceforward still continue to be accomplished, notwithstanding all the ineffectual opposition of the gates of hell; so that the elect in due time may be gathered together into one, and that there may always be a church composed of believers, the foundation of which is laid in the blood of Christ; which may steadfastly love and faithfully serve Him as its Savior (who, as a bridegroom for his bride, laid down His life for them upon the cross); and which may celebrate His praises here and through all eternity.

So, for whom did Christ die?

Does believing in a "limited" atonement cause us to be disinterested and passionless in evangelism?

Canons of Dort II,5

> Moreover, the promise of the gospel is that whosoever believes in Christ crucified shall not perish, but have eternal life. This promise, together with the command to repent and believe, ought to be declared and published to all nations, and to all persons promiscuously and without distinction, to whom God out of His good pleasure sends the gospel.

The Death of Christ

We now confess what God the Son, specifically, has done to secure our salvation by becoming a high priest to satisfy the eternal wrath of God as the ground, or, foundation, of our salvation. As our priest, he placed himself on the altar as the sacrifice for our sins.

Because of this marvelous truth, we receive unspeakable comfort and peace to give us confidence before God, as article 21, "Of the Satisfaction of Christ for our Sins," says,

> We believe that Jesus Christ is ordained with an oath to be an everlasting High Priest, after the order of Melchizedek; and that He has presented Himself in our behalf before the Father, to appease His wrath by His full satisfaction, by offering Himself on the tree of the cross, and pouring out His precious blood to purge away our sins, as the prophets had foretold. For it is written: *He was wounded for our transgressions, he was bruised for our iniquities; the chastisement of our peace was upon him; and with his stripes we are healed. He was led as a lamb to the slaughter, and numbered with the transgressors*; and condemned by Pontius Pilate as a malefactor, though he had first declared Him innocent. Therefore, He *restored that which he took not away*, and *suffered, the righteous for the unrighteous*, as well in His body and in His soul, feeling the terrible punishment which our sins had merited; insomuch that *his sweat became as it were great drops of blood falling down upon the ground*. He called out: *My God, my God, why hast thou forsaken me?* and has suffered all this for the remission of our sins.
>
> Therefore we justly say with the apostle Paul that we know nothing *save Jesus Christ, and him crucified*; we *count all things but loss and refuse for the excellency of the knowledge of Christ Jesus our Lord*, in whose wounds we find all manner of consolation. Neither is it necessary to seek or invent any other means of being reconciled to God than this only sacrifice, once offered, by which *he hath perfected forever them that are sanctified*. This is also the reason

The Death of Christ

why He was called by the angel of God, JESUS, that is to say, SAVIOR, because He would *save his people from their sins.*

Reflection Question

Is the idea of the crucifixion of Jesus for sins still relevant to the world today?

Study Questions

What does it mean that Jesus Christ "appeased" God's wrath?

Why is it not necessary to seek or invent another means of reconciliation? (see below)

Heidelberg Catechism, Q&A 29

Why is the Son of God called "Jesus," that is, Savior?

Because He saves us from all our sins, and because salvation is not to be sought or found in any other.

Heidelberg Catechism, Q&A 30

Do those also believe in the only Savior Jesus, who seek their salvation and welfare from "saints," themselves, or anywhere else?

No; although they make their boast of Him, yet in their deeds they deny the only Savior Jesus; for either Jesus is not a complete Savior, or they who by true faith receive this Savior, must have in Him all that is necessary to their salvation.

The Good Confession

What comfort do we receive from Christ's sacrifice for us? (see below)

Heidelberg Catechism, Q&A 37

What do you understand by the word "suffered?"

That all the time He lived on earth, but especially at the end of His life, He bore, in body and soul, the wrath of God against the sin of the whole human race; in order that by His suffering, as the only atoning sacrifice, He might redeem our body and soul from everlasting damnation, and obtain for us the grace of God, righteousness, and eternal life.

Heidelberg Catechism, Q&A 38

Why did He suffer "under Pontius Pilate" as judge?

That He, being innocent, might be condemned by the temporal judge, and thereby deliver us from the severe judgment of God, to which we were exposed.

Heidelberg Catechism, Q&A 39

Is there anything more in His having been "crucified" than if He had suffered some other death?

Yes, for thereby I am assured that He took upon Himself the curse which lay upon me, because the death of the cross was accursed of God.

Heidelberg Catechism, Q&A 40

Why was it necessary for Christ to suffer "death?"

Because the justice and truth of God required that satisfaction for our sins could be made in no other way than by the death of the Son of God.

Heidelberg Catechism, Q&A 41

> Why was He "buried?"
>
> To show thereby that He was really dead.

Heidelberg Catechism, Q&A 42

> Since, then, Christ died for us, why must we also die?
>
> Our death is not a satisfaction for our sin, but only a dying to sin and an entering into eternal life.

Heidelberg Catechism, Q&A 43

> What further benefit do we receive from the sacrifice and death of Christ on the cross?
>
> That by His power our old man is with Him crucified, slain, and buried; so that the evil lusts of the flesh may no more reign in us, but that we may offer ourselves unto Him a sacrifice of thanksgiving.

Heidelberg Catechism, Q&A 44

> Why is it added: "He descended into hell?"
>
> That in my greatest temptations I may be assured that Christ my Lord, by His inexpressible anguish, pains, and terrors, which He suffered in His soul on the cross and before, has redeemed me from the anguish and torment of hell.

For Further Study

On *Belgic Confession* articles 20–21 see Daniel Hyde, "We Confess: Article 20." *The Outlook* 55:2 (February 2005): 5–7 and Daniel Hyde, "We Confess: Article 21." *The Outlook* 55:3 (March 2005): 5–8.

On the atonement, see *Putting Amazing Back Into Grace*, 85–119.

11

Justification

Justification by Faith Alone

BECAUSE EACH Person of the Holy Trinity works together with the other two Persons, we confess that the Holy Spirit, also, has done a marvelous work to secure our salvation. What has he done for us? He has given us the faith by which we are able to receive Jesus Christ's righteousness. Thus, we are justified. Moreover, because we receive Christ alone by faith alone, our salvation is a complete and sufficient salvation, based solely on the work of Christ, whose obedience, merit, and works are more than sufficient to forgive and to declare righteous. Article 22, "Of Justifying Faith and the Justification of Faith," says,

> We believe that, to attain the true knowledge of this great mystery, the Holy Spirit kindles in our hearts an upright faith, which embraces Jesus Christ with all His merits, appropriates Him, and seeks nothing more besides Him. For it must needs follow, either that all things which are requisite to our salvation are not in Jesus Christ, or if all things are in Him, that then those who posses Jesus Christ through faith have complete salvation in Him. Therefore, for any to assert that Christ is not sufficient, but that something more is required besides Him, would be to gross a blasphemy; for hence it would follow that Christ was but half a Savior.
>
> Therefore we justly say with Paul, that we *are justified by faith* alone, or *by faith apart from works*. However, to speak more clearly, we do not mean that faith itself justifies us, for it is only an instrument with which we embrace Christ our righteousness. But Jesus Christ, imputing to us all His merits, and so many holy works which He has done for us and in our stead, is our righteousness. And faith is an instrument that keeps us in communion with Him in all His benefits, which, when they become ours, are more than sufficient to acquit us of our sins.

The Good Confession

What is the meaning of all that we have confessed in articles 20–22? It means that we are justified—right with God! Yet, what does justification mean? Furthermore, how should the knowledge and experience of this verdict of God affect our lives? It means that we do not need to seek another means of salvation while it also means that we can stand in full assurance before God, without fear. "Of the Justice by Which We Stand Before God" is the title of article 23, which says,

> We believe that our salvation consists in the remission of our sins for Jesus Christ's sake, and that therein our righteousness before God is implied; as David and Paul teach us, declaring this to be the blessedness of man that *God imputes righteousness to him apart from works*. And the same apostle says that we are *justified freely by his grace, through the redemption that is in Christ Jesus*.
>
> And therefore we always hold fast this foundation, ascribing all the glory to God, humbling ourselves before Him, and acknowledging ourselves to be as we really are, without presuming to trust in any thing in ourselves, or in any merit of ours, relying and resting upon the obedience of Christ crucified alone, which becomes ours when we believe in Him. This is sufficient to cover all our iniquities, and to give us confidence in approaching to God; freeing the conscience of fear, terror, and dread, without following the example of our first father, Adam, who, trembling, attempted to cover himself with fig-leaves. And, verily, if we should appear before God, relying on ourselves or on any other creature, though ever so little, we should, alas! be consumed. And therefore every one must pray with David: *O Jehovah, enter not into judgment with thy servant: for in thy sight no man living is righteous*.

Reflection Question

Compare and contrast the world's view that "as long as you have faith you are fine" with that of Scripture and the *Confession* above.

Justification

STUDY QUESTIONS

What is the Holy Spirit's primary role in our salvation?

What is true faith? (see below)

Heidelberg Catechism, Q&A 21

> It is not only a certain knowledge, whereby I accept as true all that God has revealed to us in His Word; but also a deep-rooted assurance, created in me by the Holy Spirit through the Gospel, that not only to others, but to me also, forgiveness of sins, everlasting righteousness and salvation, are freely given by God, merely of grace, for the sake of Christ's merits.

Heidelberg Catechism, Q&A 21 (above) gives the traditional three "parts" of true faith. Can you find them and name them?

1.

2.

3.

Who gives us this faith? (Eph 2:8; *Heidelberg Catechism,* Q&A 65; *Canons of Dort* III/IV, 14)

What is the way in which this faith is created in us? (Rom 10:13–17; *Heidelberg Catechism,* Q&A 65)

The Good Confession

What does faith do? (see below)

Heidelberg Catechism, Q&A 20

>Are all men, then, saved by Christ as they have perished in Adam?
>
>No, only those who by true faith are ingrafted into Him and receive all His benefits.

Why is the righteousness of Jesus Christ sufficient to forgive and to declare righteous? (see below)

>Our unworthiness is covered and swallowed up by the holiness of Jesus Christ, which is far more powerful to sanctify us before God than natural corruption is to pollute us.[1]

What is "justification?" (see below)

Heidelberg Catechism, Q&A 60

>How are you righteous before God?
>
>Only by true faith in Jesus Christ: that is, although my conscience accuses me, that I have grievously sinned against all the commandments of God, and have never kept any of them, and am still prone always to all evil; yet God, without any merit of mine, of mere grace, grants and imputes to me the perfect satisfaction, righteousness, and holiness of Christ, as if I had never committed nor had any sins, and had myself accomplished all the obedience which Christ has fulfilled for me; if only I accept such benefit with a believing heart.

---

[1] Beza, *The Christian Faith*, 23.

Justification

What is the way in which we become justified? (Rom 1:17, 3:21–26, 28, 4:1–8; *Heidelberg Catechism*, Q&A 60–61)

What is the "ground," or basis, on which we are justified? (Rom 5:12–19; see below)

Heidelberg Catechism, Q&A 61

Why do you say that you are righteous by faith only?

Not that I am acceptable to God on account of the worthiness of my faith, but because only the satisfaction, righteousness and holiness of Christ is my righteousness before God; and I can receive the same and make it my own in no other way than by faith only.

For Further Study

On *Belgic Confession* articles 22–23 see Daniel Hyde, "We Confess: Article 22." *The Outlook* 55:4 (April 2005): 5–7 and Daniel Hyde, "We Confess: Article 23." *The Outlook* 55:5 (May 2005): 7–10.

On justification, see Horton, *Putting Amazing Back Into Grace*, 120–49.

12

Sanctification

REFLECTION QUESTION

What is the relationship between being a Christian and living a godly life? Are Christians better people than non-Christians?

Sanctification

As we said above, Christ has merited two great benefits for us: justification and sanctification. By earning for us justification, we are no longer under the guilt of sin. However, the drama does not end there. It continues as we see that by earning for us sanctification, Christ has made us new creatures who are becoming more and more like Jesus, as we are renewed in the image of God by the powerful working of the Holy Spirit.

We confess also the relationship between justification and sanctification. Good works have no standing before God for our justification; rather, they are the logical and necessary response to justification. This is what article 24, "Of Sanctification and of Good Works," says,

> We believe that this true faith, being wrought in man by the hearing of the Word of God and the operation of the Holy Spirit, regenerates him and makes him a new man, causing him to live a new life, and freeing him from the bondage of sin. Therefore it is so far from being true that this justifying faith makes men remiss in a pious and holy life, that on the contrary without it they would never do anything out of love to God, but only out of self-love or fear of damnation. Therefore it is impossible that this holy faith to be unfruitful in man; for we do not speak of a vain faith, but

of such a faith which is called in Scripture a *faith working through love*, which excites man to the practice of those works which God has commanded in His Word.

These works, as they proceed from the good root of faith, are good and acceptable in the sight of God, forasmuch as they are all sanctified by His grace. Nevertheless they are of no account towards our justification, for it is by faith in Christ that we are justified, even before we do good works; otherwise they could not be good works, any more than the fruit of a tree can be good before the tree itself is good.

Therefore we do good works, but not to merit by them (for what can we merit?); nay, we are indebted to God for the good works we do, and not He to us, since it is He who *worketh in us both to will and to work, for his good pleasure*. Let us therefore attend to what is written: *When ye shall have done all the things that are commanded you, say, We are unprofitable servants; we have done that which it was our duty to do*. In the meantime we do not deny that God rewards good works, but it is through His grace that He crowns His gifts.

Moreover, though we do good works, we do not found our salvation upon them; for we can do no work but what is polluted by our flesh, and also punishable; and although we could perform such works, still the remembrance of one sin is sufficient to make God reject them. Thus, then, we would always be in doubt, tossed to and fro without any certainty, and our poor consciences would be continually vexed if they relied not on the merits of the suffering and death of our Savior.

Heidelberg Catechism, Q&A 86

Since, then, we are redeemed from our misery by grace through Christ, without any merit of ours, why must we do good works?

Because Christ, having redeemed us by His blood, also renews us by His Holy Spirit after His own image, that with our whole life we show ourselves thankful to God for His blessing, and that He be glorified through us; then also, that we ourselves may be assured by our faith by the fruits thereof; and by our godly walk win also others to Christ.

Sanctification

STUDY QUESTIONS

Define sanctification.

What does it mean to be "regenerated?"
(*Canons of Dort* III/IV, 10–13, 16)

Does knowing that we are justified by faith alone, and not by our works, cause us to want to sin more? Why or why not?
(Rom 5:20–6:2; see below)

Heidelberg Catechism, Q&A 63

> Do our good works merit nothing, even though it is God's will to reward them in this life and in that which is to come?
>
> The reward comes not of merit, but of grace.

Heidelberg Catechism, Q&A 64

> But does not this doctrine make men careless and profane?
>
> No, for it is impossible that those who are implanted into Christ by true faith, should not bring forth fruits of thankfulness.

Heidelberg Catechism, Q&A 88

> In how many things does true repentance or conversion consist?
>
> In two things: the dying of the old man, and the making alive of the new.

Heidelberg Catechism, Q&A 89

> What is the dying of the old man?
>
> Heartfelt sorrow for sin, causing us to hate and turn from it always more and more.

Heidelberg Catechism, Q&A 90

> What is the making alive of the new man?
>
> Heartfelt joy in God through Christ, causing us to take delight in living according to the will of God in all good works.

Heidelberg Catechism, Q&A 91

> What are good works?
>
> Those only which proceed from true faith, and are done according to the Law of God, unto His glory, and not such as rest on our own opinion or the commandments of men.

What does the analogy of the tree and its roots
have to do with sanctification?

Why are we not to look to our good works when our faith
is weak or we are in doubt? (see below)

Heidelberg Catechism, Q&A 62

> But why cannot our good works be the whole or part of our righteousness before God?
>
> Because the righteousness which can stand before the judgment seat of God, must be perfect throughout and entirely conformable to the divine law, but even our best works in this life are all imperfect and defiled with sin.

Sanctification

Heidelberg Catechism, Q&A 87

> Can they, then, not be saved who do not turn to God from their unthankful, impenitent life?
>
> By no means, for, as Scripture says, no unchaste person, idolater, adulterer, thief, covetous man, drunkard, slanderer, robber, or the like shall inherit the kingdom of God.

The Christian Use of the Old Testament Law

As new creatures in Christ we begin to perform those "works which God has commanded in His Word." Here in article 25, "Of the Abrogation of the Ceremonial Law and the Agreement of the Old and New Testaments," we confess where the Word of God commands us to do good works—in the law of God. So then, what is the role of the law in the Christian life? It no longer condemns us or enslaves us; instead, it serves us as a guide to lead us in a life of holiness before the Lord. Thus the classic Protestant distinction between the Law and the Gospel is confessed:

> We believe that the ceremonies and symbols of the law ceased at the coming of Christ, and that all the shadows are accomplished; so that the use of them must be abolished among Christians; yet the truth and substance of them remain with us in Jesus Christ, in whom they have their completion. In the meantime we still use the testimonies taken out of the law and the prophets to confirm us in the doctrine of the gospel, and to regulate our life in all honorableness to the glory of God, according to His will.

Reflection Question

In your own words, how does the Old Testament
relate to the New Testament?

The Good Confession

Study Questions

In classic Reformed theology, the Law of God has a threefold *division*. First, there is the moral aspect of the law. This means everything in the law that expresses an abiding principle of who God is and who we are to be. Second, there are the ceremonial aspects of the law, which are those things that teach some religious truth thereby leading the people to the Messiah, Jesus Christ. Third, there is the judicial aspect, which are those punishments given in the law.

Read Exodus 20:8–11 and 31:12–18.
Which aspect of the Sabbath commandment was:

1. Moral

2. Ceremonial

3. Judicial

Which division of the Law is relevant to the Church?
Which division is not?

As well, in classic Reformed theology, we understand that the Law of God has three "uses." First, there is the pedagogical use (Latin, *usus pedagogicus*). This means that the law is a "tutor" to lead us to Christ by showing us our sins and our futile efforts to save ourselves (Gal 3:24). Second, there is the civil use (Latin, *usus civilis*), which is the law used in society. This is the law written on the heart of man as well as using the general principles in the law to restrain society from unbridled wickedness. Third, there is the didactic use (Latin, *usus didacticus*), which we oftentimes call the "third use" of the law. This is the law used as a guide for gratitude as we respond to Christ's amazing grace.

Heidelberg Catechism, Q&A 114

Can those who are converted to God keep these Commandments perfectly?

Sanctification

No, but even the holiest men, while in this life, have only a small beginning of such obedience, yet so that with earnest purpose they begin to live not only according to some, but according to all the Commandments of God.

Heidelberg Catechism, Q&A 115

Why then does God so strictly enjoin the Ten Commandments upon us, since in this life no one can keep them?

First, that as long as we live we may learn more and more to know our sinful nature, and so the more earnestly seek forgiveness of sins and righteousness in Christ; second, that without ceasing we diligently ask God for the grace of the Holy Spirit, that we be renewed more and more after the image of God, until we attain the goal of perfection after this life.

STUDY QUESTIONS (*continued*)

Can the Law save us? (*Canons of Dort* III/IV, 5)
Why or why not?

Why is it so important to correctly distinguish between the Law and the Gospel?

What is the role of the Ten Commandments in the Christian life? (*Heidelberg Catechism*, Q&A 86, 90, 91, 114, 115)

The Good Confession

Read the Ten Commandments (Exod 20; Deut 5) and summarize what they teach you about the Christian life in your own words:

1st Commandment (Heidelberg Catechism, Q&A 94–95)

2nd Commandment (Heidelberg Catechism, Q&A 96–98)

3rd Commandment (Heidelberg Catechism, Q&A 99–102)

4th Commandment (Heidelberg Catechism, Q&A 103)

5th Commandment (Heidelberg Catechism, Q&A 104)

6th Commandment (Heidelberg Catechism, Q&A 105–107)

7th Commandment (Heidelberg Catechism, Q&A 108–109)

8th Commandment (Heidelberg Catechism, Q&A 110–111)

9th Commandment (Heidelberg Catechism, Q&A 112)

Sanctification

10th Commandment (Heidelberg Catechism, Q&A 113)

The Lord's Day

The Lord's Day is the central hub of the Christian life, from which we live our lives as a community of Christians. We set aside the Lord's Day for public worship with the people of God. The Reformed Churches have always followed the ancient Jewish and Christian practice of having worship twice on the Lord's Day, in the morning and evening. Why is the Lord's Day so important for our Christian life? It is because here we receive the means of grace, preaching and sacraments, as well as the fellowship of the saints during worship and after. We assemble with expectance to hear from God on this day. We come with an expectation to receive the grace of God in the sacraments. We come with an eagerness to praise God. We come with an expectation to fellowship with the people of God.

Read the following Scripture passages and quoted *Heidelberg Catechism* question and answer: Exodus 20:8–11, 31:12–17, Deuteronomy 5:12–15, Isaiah 58:13–14, Mark 2:23–28, Acts 2:42–47, Hebrews 10:19–25.

Heidelberg Catechism, Q&A 103

> What does God require in the fourth commandment?
>
> In the first place, that the ministry of the Gospel and schools be maintained; and that I, especially on the day of rest, diligently attend Church to learn the Word of God, to use the Holy Sacraments, to call publicly upon the Lord, and to give Christian alms. In the second place, that all the days of my life I rest from my evil works, allow the Lord to work in me by His Spirit, and thus begin in this life the everlasting Sabbath.

Study Questions

Why did God give us the Sabbath/Lord's Day?

The Good Confession

What two things are we to remember on the Lord's Day?

1.

2.

Why do we meet on Sunday and not Saturday?

Is the New Testament Lord's Day the same as the Old Testament Sabbath?

The Synod of Dort (1618–19) adopted the following six points in its 164th Session. They give a good summary of the Reformed position on the Lord's Day.

1. There is in the fourth commandment of the divine law a ceremonial and a moral element.

2. The ceremonial element is the rest of the seventh day after creation, and the strict observance of that day imposed especially on the Jewish people.

3. The moral element consists in the fact that a certain definite day is set aside for worship and so much rest as is needful for worship and hallowed meditation.

4. The Sabbath of the Jews having been abolished, the day of the Lord must be solemnly hallowed by Christians.

5. Since the times of the apostles this day has always been observed by the old catholic church.

6. This day must be so consecrated to worship that on that day we rest from all servile works, except those which charity and present necessity require; and also from all such recreations as interfere with worship.

For Further Study

On *Belgic Confession* articles 24–25 see Daniel Hyde, "We Confess: Articles 24–25." *The Outlook* 55:6 (June 2005): 9–11 and Daniel Hyde, "We Confess: Article 25." *The Outlook* 55:7 (July/August 2005): 10–11.

13

Preservation/Perseverance

Reflection Question

What do you think about the phrase,
"Once saved always saved?"

Christ's Preservation Through Intercession

WE CONCLUDE this part of the drama of our redemption as we stand back and acknowledge that there is only one great high priest over the house of God, the Church: the Lord Jesus Christ. As our merciful and faithful high priest, he continues to pray for us even now as those who are simultaneously justified and sinful, saints and sinners. This article is a marvelous summary of the Reformation's re-discovery of Jesus Christ being the Church's ever-living intercessor before the throne of God. Article 26, "Of Christ's Intercession," details this belief by saying,

> We believe that we have no access unto God but alone through the only Mediator and Advocate Jesus Christ the righteous; who therefore became man, having united in one person the divine and human natures, that we men might have access to the divine Majesty, which access would otherwise be barred against us. But this Mediator, whom the Father has appointed between Him and us, ought in no wise to affright us by His majesty, or cause us to seek another according to our fancy. For there is no creature, either in heaven or on earth, who loves us more than Jesus Christ; who, though *existing in the form of God,* yet *emptied himself, being made in the likeness of man and of a servant* for us, and *in all things was made like unto his brethren.* If, then, we should seek for another

mediator who would be favorably inclined towards us, whom could we find who loved us more than He who laid down His life for us, even *while we were His enemies*? And if we seek for one who has power and majesty, who is there that has so much of both as He *who sits at the right hand of God* and *to whom hath been given all authority in heaven and on earth*? And who will sooner be heard than the own well beloved Son of God?

Therefore it was only through distrust that this practice of dishonoring, instead of honoring, the saints was introduced, doing that which they never have done nor required, but have on the contrary steadfastly rejected according to their bounden duty, as appears by their writings. Neither must we plead here our unworthiness; for the meaning is not that we should offer our prayers to God on the ground of our own worthiness, but only on the ground of the excellency and worthiness of the Lord Jesus Christ, whose righteousness is become ours by faith.

Therefore the apostle, to remove this foolish fear, or rather distrust, from us, rightly says that Jesus Christ *in all things was made like unto his brethren, that he might become a merciful and faithful high priest, to make propitiation for the sins of the people. For in that he himself hath suffered being tempted, he is able to succor them that are tempted*. And further to encourage us to go to Him, he says: *Having then a great high priest, who hath passed through the heavens, Jesus the Son of God, let us hold fast our confession. For we have not a high priest that cannot be touched with the feeling of our infirmities; but one that hath been in all points tempted like as* we are, yet *without sin. Let us therefore draw near with boldness unto the throne of grace, that we may receive mercy, and may find grace to help us in time of need*. The same apostle says: *Having boldness to enter into the holy place by the blood of Jesus, let us draw near with a true heart in fullness of faith*, etc. Likewise: Christ *hath his priesthood unchangeable; wherefore also he is able to save to the uttermost them that draw near unto God through him, seeing he ever liveth to make intercession for them*.

What more can be required? since Christ Himself says: *I am the way, and the truth, and the life; no one cometh unto the Father, but by me*. To what purpose should we, then, seek another advocate, since it has pleased God to give us His own Son as an Advocate? Let us not forsake Him to take another, or rather to seek after another, without ever being able to find him; for God well knew, when He gave Him to us, that we were sinners.

Therefore, according to the command of Christ, we call upon the heavenly Father through Jesus Christ our only Mediator, as we

Preservation/Perseverance

are taught in the Lord's Prayer; being assured that whatever we ask of the Father in His Name will be granted us.

Study Questions

Why does the *Confession* spend an entire article, and a very long one at that, on the subject of Christ's intercession?

How does Christ's intercession relate to our justification and sanctification? (Heb 7:25; see below)

Heidelberg Catechism, Q&A 49

> First, that He is our Advocate in the presence of His Father in heaven. Second, that we have our flesh in heaven as a sure pledge, that He as the Head, will also take us, His members, up to Himself. Third, that He sends us His Spirit as an earnest, by whose power we seek those things which are above, where Christ sits at the right hand of God, and not things on the earth.

What do we mean when we speak of the perseverance/preservation of the saints? (see below)

Canons of Dort, V, 3

> By reason of these remains of indwelling sin, and also because of the temptations of the world and of Satan, those who are converted could not persevere in that grace if left to their own strength. But God is faithful, who, having conferred grace, mercifully confirms and powerfully preserves them therein, even to the end.

Canons of Dort, V, 6

> But God, who is rich in mercy, according to His unchangeable purpose of election, does not wholly withdraw the Holy Spirit from His own people even in their grievous falls; nor does He allow them to proceed so far as to lose the grace of adoption and

forfeit the state of justification, or to commit the sin unto death or against the Holy Spirit; nor does He permit them to be totally deserted and plunge themselves into everlasting destruction.

Canons of Dort, V, 7

For in the first place, in these falls He preserves in them the incorruptible seed of regeneration from perishing or being totally lost; and again, by His Word and Spirit He certainly and effectually renews them to repentance, to a sincere and godly sorrow for their sins, that they may seek and obtain remission in the blood of the Mediator, may again experience the favor of a reconciled God, through faith adore His mercies, and henceforward more diligently work out their own salvation with fear and trembling.

Canons of Dort, V, 8

Thus it is not in consequence of their own merits or strength, but of God's free mercy, that they neither totally fall from faith and grace nor continue and perish finally in their backslidings; which, with respect to themselves is not only possible, but would undoubtedly happen; but with respect to God, it is utterly impossible, since His counsel cannot be changed nor His promise fail; neither can the call according to His purpose be revoked, nor the merit, intercession, and preservation of Christ be rendered ineffectual, nor the sealing of the Holy Spirit be frustrated or obliterated.

> Describe your attitude to the grace of salvation from beginning to end. In other words, does the knowledge that *God* preserves his people cause spiritual laziness, even licentiousness? (see below)

Canons of Dort, V, 12

This certainty of perseverance, however, is so far from exciting in believers a spirit of pride, or of rendering them carnally secure, that on the contrary it is the real source of humility, filial reverence, true piety, patience in every tribulation, fervent prayers, constancy in suffering and in confessing the truth, and of solid rejoicing in God; so that the consideration of this benefit should serve as an incentive to the serious and constant practice of gratitude and good works, as appears from the testimonies of Scripture and the examples of the saints.

Canons of Dort, V, 13

Neither does renewed confidence of persevering produce licentiousness or a disregard of piety in those who are recovered from backsliding; but it renders them much more careful and concerned to continue in the ways of the Lord, which He has ordained that they who walk therein may keep the assurance of persevering; lest, on account of their abuse of His fatherly kindness, God should turn away His gracious countenance from them (which is to the godly dearer than life, and the withdrawal of which is more bitter than death) and they in consequence thereof should fall into more grievous torments of conscience.

Why do we emphasize the biblical teaching that there is only one Mediator between God and man? (1 Tim 2:5)

In and of ourselves, we are unworthy to approach God. Therefore, how are we to "boldly approach the throne of grace?" (Heb 4:16, 10:19–20)

What is the role of prayer in the Christian life? (see below)

Heidelberg Catechism, Q&A 116

Why is prayer necessary for Christians?
Because it is the chief part of thankfulness which God requires of us, and because God will give His grace and Holy Spirit only to those who earnestly and without ceasing ask them of Him, and render thanks unto Him for them.

The Good Confession

Heidelberg Catechism, Q&A 117

What belongs to such prayer which is acceptable to God and which He will hear?

First, that with our whole heart we call only upon the one true God, who has revealed Himself to us in His Word, for all that He has commanded us to ask of Him; second, that we thoroughly know our need and misery, so as to humble ourselves in the presence of His divine majesty; third, that we be firmly assured that notwithstanding our unworthiness He will, for the sake of Christ our Lord, certainly hear our prayer, as He has promised us in His Word.

Heidelberg Catechism, Q&A 118

What has God commanded us to ask of Him?

All things necessary for soul and body, which Christ our Lord comprised in the prayer which He Himself taught us.

> How does the following statement from the *Confession* comfort you: "for God well knew, when He gave Him to us, that we were sinners?"

For Further Study

On *Belgic Confession* article 26 see Daniel Hyde, "We Confess: Article 26." *The Outlook* 55:8 (September 2005): 7–10.

On sanctification and the Christian life being defined by the biblical metaphor of pilgrimage, see Daniel Hyde, "The Pilgrim's Progress." *The Presbyterian Banner* (November 2003): 8–9.

On the preservation/perseverance of the saints, see Horton, *Putting Amazing Back Into Grace*, 150–60.

14

The Church: Part 1

One of the most powerful reasons for our lack of gladness is that ours is a culture of solo efforts. We live our Christian faith independently—not inextricably linked with other members of the Body of believers. Consequently, we do not experience the Hilarity of being enfolded in a moment-by-moment awareness of the good news of our hope and life in Jesus Christ. We don't experience the support that true community engenders . . . So I use the word Hilarity to describe the ideal Christian community, and my intention is to make us stop and think: what would it be like if the Christian Church were truly a community that thoroughly enjoyed being itself? It seems to me it could change the world!
(Marva Dawn)[1]

Reflection Question

How important is the Church?

IN DISCUSSING our redemption from the fall into sin, we have looked at the Person of the Redeemer, the God-man, Jesus Christ the Lord, as well as the method of our redemption: the obedience and death of Christ, which we receive as the satisfaction for our sins by faith alone.

This dramatic portrayal of our redemption continues in articles 27–35 as we confess the place in which this redemption is found, the Church, and the means by which we are sustained in that redemption until the

---

[1] *Truly the Community: Romans 12 and How to Be the Church* (Grand Rapids: Eerdmans, reprinted 1997), xi.

consummation, the word and sacraments. Our drama turns, then, from *theology proper*, *anthropology*, *Christology*, and *soteriology* to *ecclesiology*, the doctrine of the Church. It is a telling fact that 10 out of our *Confession of Faith's* 37 articles deal with this topic. We confess the nature (arts. 27–29), government (arts. 30–32), and sacraments of the Church (arts. 33–35), as well as the relationship between the Church and the State (art. 36).[2]

A Holy Catholic Church

The drama of the dogma is not an individualistic drama, but one in which together we join. The Father has sent his Son to redeem a people (plural) for himself, the Church. This salvation has an individual dimension, to be true, as we have already seen, but it also has a corporate dimension. Here in article 27, "Of the Catholic Church," we learn the meaning of the *Apostles' Creed's* confession, "I believe a holy catholic Church." We as Reformed churches confess to believe that we are the continuation of the true "catholic" Church:

> We believe and profess one catholic or universal Church, which is a holy congregation of true Christian believers, all expecting their salvation in Jesus Christ, being washed by His blood, sanctified and sealed by the Holy Spirit.
>
> This Church has been from the beginning of the world, and will be to the end thereof; which is evident from this that Christ is an eternal King, which without subjects He cannot be.
>
> And this holy Church is preserved or supported by God against the rage of the whole world; though it sometimes for a while appears very small, and in the eyes of men to be reduced to nothing; as during the perilous reign of Ahab the Lord reserved unto Him seven thousand men who had not bowed their knees to Baal.
>
> Furthermore, this holy Church is not confined, bound, or limited to a certain place or to certain persons, but is spread and dispersed over the whole world; and yet is joined and united with heart and will, by the power of faith, in one and the same Spirit.

Heidelberg Catechism, Q&A 54

> What do you believe concerning the "holy catholic Church?"
>
> That out of the whole human race, from the beginning to the end of the world, the Son of God, by His Spirit and Word, gathers, defends, and preserves for Himself unto everlasting life a chosen

---

[2] We will not discuss article 36 of the *Belgic Confession* in this workbook.

The Church: Part 1

communion in the unity of the true faith; and that I am and forever shall remain a living member of this communion.

STUDY QUESTIONS

In the *Nicene Creed*, we confess that the Church is "one, holy, catholic, and apostolic." Now is a good time to discuss the Reformed understanding of these attributes of the Church:

1. What is the meaning of one? (Eph 4:4)

2. What is the meaning of holy? (Eph 2:21, 5:26–27)

3. What is the meaning of catholic? (Matt 11:27; Acts 10:27–28; Rev 5:9, 7:9)

4. What is the meaning of apostolic? (Eph 2:20)

When did the Church begin? (*Heidelberg Catechism*, Q&A 54)
What is the proof the *Confession* gives for this?
(2 Sam 7:16; Luke 1:32–33; Pss 89:37; 110)

Can the Church be destroyed? (Matt 16:18)

What does the *Confession* and 1 Kings 19 say about how "successful" the church is in the eyes of the world?

The Communion of Saints

We believe there is a Church, a congregation of those whom the Lord has saved. Just as the early Christians devoted themselves to the apostles' doctrine and to the Lord's Supper and prayer, so they were devoted to each other, "*the* fellowship" (Acts 2:42). We see this described by the metaphor of a body in Paul's words in Romans 12, where Paul says that a body has many "members." We as the members of the body are one body in Christ. Even more striking is Paul's conclusion—because we are members of Christ, we are "members one of another."

In article 28 of our *Belgic Confession*, "Of the Communion of the Saints in the True Church," we confess that we are members of that Church, a part of the "communion of the saints":

> We believe, since this holy congregation is an assembly of those who are saved, and outside of it there is no salvation, that no person of whatsoever state or condition he may be, ought to withdraw from it, content to be by himself; but that all men are in duty bound to join and unite themselves with it; maintain the unity of the Church; submitting themselves to the doctrine and discipline thereof; bowing their necks under the yoke of Jesus Christ; and as mutual members of the same body, serving to the edification of the brethren, according to the talents God has given them.
>
> And that this may be more effectively observed, it is the duty of all believers, according to the Word of God, to separate themselves from all those who do not belong to the Church, and to join themselves to this congregation, wheresoever God has established it, even though the magistrates and edicts of princes were against it, yea, though they should suffer death or any other corporal punishment. Therefore all those who separate themselves from the same or do not join themselves to it act contrary to the ordinance of God.

Heidelberg Catechism, Q&A 55

> What do you understand by the "communion of saints?"
>
> First, that *believers, one and all, as members of the Lord Jesus Christ*, are partakers with Him in all His treasures and gifts; second, that *each one must feel himself bound to use his gifts readily and cheerfully for the advantage and welfare of other members*.

The Church: Part 1

Reflection Question

In biblical metaphors, God is Father, Christ is Son,
and we are sons of God and fellow brothers/sisters.
What, then, does it mean to say the Church is mother?

Study Questions

What do we mean by the shocking statement, "Outside the
church there is no salvation?" (Rom 10:14–17; Eph 2:11–22)

Why can a true Christian not be a "lone ranger" in the world?
(Heb 10:24–25)

The *Confession of Faith* speaks of the obligation of "joining"
the visible church. Is this biblical? Is it necessary?
Explain your answers.

What do the following metaphors for the Church teach us
about membership in the Church?

Vine/Branches (John 15)

Shepherd/Sheep (John 10)

Temple/Stones (1 Pet 2)

Body/Members (Rom 12)

Bride/Husband (Eph 5)

What does it mean to be a "member" of Christ's Church? Although many people, even Christians, associate membership with strictness, or a controlling environment, or with the loss of Christian freedom, biblical church membership could not be further from these ideas. As we will see, to unite ourselves not only with our lips to Christ but to his Church with our lives entails both great responsibilities and great blessings.

Responsibilities/Blessings of Membership

Historic Christian churches follow the practice of the earliest Christians in taking sacred oaths/vows before God and his Church when someone unites him/herself to the Church (remember our comments on Ephesians 4:4–6 and the *Apostles' Creed*). In doing this believers unite themselves publicly to Jesus Christ as well as to his Body, their fellow members of Christ.

One example of the vows a believer takes in uniting with a local church are those of the "Form for the Public Profession of Faith," which many Reformed congregations use:[3]

> First, do you heartily believe the doctrine contained in the Old and the New Testament, and in the articles of the Christian Faith, and taught in this Christian Church, to be the true and complete doctrine of salvation, and do you promise by the grace of God steadfastly to continue in this profession?
>
> Second, do you openly accept God's covenant promise, which has been signified and sealed unto you in your baptism, and do you confess that you abhor and humble yourself before God because of your sins, and that you seek your life not in yourself, but only in Jesus Christ your Savior?

---

[3] These questions come from the "Form for the Public Profession of Faith" from both the 1934 and 1959 editions of the *Psalter Hymnal* (Grand Rapids: Christian Reformed Church), 86, 88. This form is known as "Public Profession of Faith: Form Number 1" in the 1976 edition of the *Psalter Hymnal*, pp. 132–133. These questions are also found in the *Book of Praise: Anglo-Genevan Psalter* (rev. ed.; Winnipeg: Premier Printing, Ltd., 1998), 593–4.

The Church: Part 1

Third, do you declare that you love the Lord, and that it is your heartfelt desire to serve Him according to His Word, to forsake the world, to mortify your old nature, and to lead a godly life?

Fourth, do you promise to submit to the government of the Church and also, if you should become delinquent either in doctrine or in life, to submit to its admonition and discipline?

Reflection on Vow #1

The first membership vow asks whether a person confesses *a common faith* with the rest of the congregation before whom they stand. When one stands before the church, they are identifying themselves with the "doctrine of the apostles" (Acts 2:42) as found in Holy Scripture and faithfully summarized in the Christian creeds and Reformed confessions. In doing so they are uniting themselves to the body of Christ locally and universally who stand and confess "the good confession."

This is an enormous blessing to stand shoulder to shoulder with others of like mind and like-precious faith. One of the blessings of membership is receiving the teaching of the pastors.

As well, this is also a responsibility. When one publicly professes faith they are not only saying they believe certain things now, but also that they will continue to believe those things. A member gives a sincere promise (covenant) that they will be faithful to their confession. This is not easy in the world in which we live; thus, members are to continue "steadfastly" in their profession.

REFLECTION QUESTIONS

What does one "heartily believe?"
(*Heidelberg Catechism*, Q&A 21)

What does it mean to heartily believe "the doctrine contained in the Old and the New Testament?"

The Good Confession

What does it mean to heartily believe "the articles of the Christian Faith" (cf. *Heidelberg Catechism*, Q&A 22, 23)?

What does it mean to heartily believe the doctrine "taught in this Christian Church?"

Reflection on Vow #2

The second membership vow asks whether a person confesses *a common salvation*. Notice that vow #2 moves from the theology that the church believes to what I believe about my salvation and myself.

Reflection Questions

What does it mean to accept the promise of God "openly"?

What is "God's covenant promise" in baptism?

Why must we "abhor and humble" ourselves?

What does it mean to seek life not in yourself but in Jesus Christ?

The Church: Part 1

Reflection on Vow #3

The third membership vow asks whether a person confesses *a common life* with the congregation, before which he stands and with whom he desires to unite. We profess that we not only believe certain things as Christians but that we will live as Christians as members of the Body of Christ. What does it mean to promise the following:

That you love the Lord—

That you desire to serve him—

That you will forsake the world—

That you will mortify your sinful nature—

That you will lead a godly life—

Reflection on Vow #4

The fourth membership vow, the most serious of the four, asks whether a person will live in submission to *a common discipline*. As we have already seen in our discussion of the elders of the church, the Lord has given the gift of rule to his church in the form of the elders, who guide the church in his place.

The blessing of discipline is being shepherded by pastors and elders. As Paul went "from house to house" (Acts 20:20) so do we as Christ's under-shepherds. In a Reformed church this means that the elders will visit you as an individual or family at least once a year in the privacy of your home to continue to get to know you better and bear each other's burdens. As well, when you are in the hospital, a pastor, elder, or deacon will visit you.

Another aspect of this shepherding is the ministry of the deacons. The duty of the deacons is to take care of the practical needs of the people, especially widows and the poor (Acts 6). If you ever are in need or know of someone who is, let the deacons know.

Reflection Questions

In vow #4, you promise to submit to the church's government in general. Please find one Scripture text that speaks of Christians submitting to the elders of the church and explain what it means.

Please explain submitting to the church's government.

This vow also is a promise to submit to the church's admonition and discipline in the specific case that you should fall in doctrine or life. For what doctrinal things can you be disciplined? What are issues of life for which you can be disciplined?

The Marks of a Church

Redemption is found in Christ, which is found in his Church, of which we are members. This is what we have said in the above two articles of our *Confession*. Yet, how do we know if a particular "church" is a church? There are so many groups in the world calling themselves "churches." The question we must answer is whether a particular church is a *true* church. Furthermore, if there are true churches, does this mean that there are false churches? As participants in this drama, we must look to the Word of God for guidance in finding a true church. Article 29, "Of the Marks of the True Church," says,

> We believe that we ought diligently and circumspectly to discern from the Word of God which is the true Church, since all sects which are in the world assume to themselves the name of the Church. But we speak not here of hypocrites, who are mixed in the Church with the good, yet are not of the Church, though externally in it; but we say that the body and communion of the true Church must be distinguished from all sects that call themselves the Church.
>
> The marks by which the true Church is known as these: If the pure doctrine of the gospel is preached therein; if it maintains the pure administration of the sacraments as instituted by Christ; if church discipline is exercised in punishing sin; in short, if all things are managed according to the pure Word of God, all things contrary thereto rejected, and Jesus Christ acknowledged as the only Head of the Church. Hereby the true Church may certainly be known, from which no man has a right to separate himself.
>
> With respect to those who are members of the Church, they may be known by the marks of Christians; namely, by faith, and when, having received Jesus Christ the only Savior, they avoid sin, follow after righteousness, love the true God and their neighbor, neither turn aside to the right or left, and crucify the flesh with the works thereof. But this is not to be understood as if there did not remain in them great infirmities; but they fight against through the Spirit all the days of their life, continually taking their refuge in the blood, death, passion, and obedience of our Lord Jesus Christ, in whom they have remission of sins, through faith in Him.
>
> As for the false Church, it ascribes more power and authority to itself and its ordinances than to the Word of God, and will not submit itself to the yoke of Christ. Neither does it administer the sacraments as appointed by Christ in His Word, but adds to and takes from them, as it thinks proper; it relies more upon men than upon Christ; and persecutes those who live holily according to the Word of God and rebuke it for its errors, covetousness, and idolatry.
>
> These two Churches are easily known and distinguished from each other.

The Good Confession

Reflection Question

Just because an assembly has the name "church" in its name, does this mean it is truly a "church?" Does this mean Christ is there?

Study Questions

How does the *Confession* describe the duty of Christians to find a true Church?

When we speak of true versus false churches, are we saying that there are no hypocrites in true churches and no believers in false churches? If not, then what does this distinction mean?

List the marks of the "true Church" below and explain each one in your own words/understanding:

1.

2.

3.

With regard to the "pure preaching of the Gospel," what does the Gospel do that the Law cannot? (*Canons of Dort* III/IV, 6)

The Church: Part 1

What characterizes a "false church?"

For Further Study

On *Belgic Confession* article 27 see Daniel Hyde, "We Confess: Article 27." *The Outlook* 55:9 (October 2005): 7–10.

On *Belgic Confession* article 28 see Daniel Hyde, "We Confess: Article 28." *The Outlook* 55:11 (December 2005): 5–8.

On *Belgic Confession* article 29 see Daniel Hyde, "We Confess: Article 29." *The Outlook* 56:1 (January 2006): 6–9.

15

The Church: Part 2

How the Church is Governed

WE KNOW that Jesus instituted a visible Church and that we are to be united to it. Since Christ is in heaven until he comes again, how is this Church to be organized and governed? In the next three articles, articles 30–32, we confess the Reformed view of church government, or, "church polity." Article 30 is entitled "Of the Government of the Church," and says,

> We believe that this true Church must be governed by that spiritual polity which our Lord has taught us in His Word; namely, that there must be ministers or pastors to preach the Word of God and to administer the sacraments; also elders and deacons, who, together with the pastors, form the council of the Church; that by these means the true religion may be preserved, and the true doctrine everywhere propagated, likewise transgressors punished and restrained by spiritual means; also that the poor and distressed may be relieved and comforted, according to their necessities. By these means everything will be carried on in the Church with good order and decency, when faithful men are chosen, according to the rule prescribed by St. Paul in his Epistle to Timothy.

REFLECTION QUESTION
Does the Bible teach "organized religion?"

The Good Confession

Study Questions

To get our thoughts started, and to give us some background, we must understand that Israel had three "offices" by which the LORD led his people. Next to each Old Testament office, write down what you think each one's purpose was:[1]

1. Prophet—

2. Priest—

3. King—

Which Old Testament office corresponds to New Testament pastors? What are the duties of pastors? (Acts 6:4, 13:2; 1 Tim 4:6, 14)

Which Old Testament office corresponds to New Testament elders? What are the duties of elders? (Acts 20:17–35; 1 Tim 3:1–7; Titus 1:5–9; Heb 13:7, 17)

Which Old Testament office corresponds to New Testament deacons? What are the duties of deacons? (Acts 6:1–6)

---

[1] For an excellent explanation of the offices of Israel and the Church, see Derke P. Bergsma, "Prophets, Priests, and Kings: Biblical Offices," in *The Compromised Church* (Wheaton: Crossway, 1998), 117–131; also Daniel R. Hyde, "Rulers and Servants: The Nature of and Qualifications for the Offices of Elder and Deacon," in *Called to Serve: Essays for Elders and Deacons,* ed. Michael G. Brown (Grandville: Reformed Fellowship, 2007).

Four terms you should know that we use as
Reformed churches:

1. Consistory (Latin, *consistorium*, "place of meeting." Called a "session" by Presbyterians)

2. Council

3. Classis (Latin, "a division or class of people or other objects." Called a "presbytery" by Presbyterians)

4. Synod (Greek, *sunodos*, "a coming together, assembly, meeting." Called a "general assembly" by Presbyterians)

The Calling of Church Officials

Pastors, elders, and deacons govern and lead the Church. The question is how do we go about electing or calling them to their respective offices. In this short article, "Of the Calling of Ministers in the Church," article 21 confesses a biblical explanation on the calling and authority of ministers, elders, and deacons:

> We believe that ministers of God's Word, the elders, and the deacons ought to be chosen to their respective offices by a lawful election by the Church, with calling upon the name of the Lord, and in that order which the Word of God teaches. Therefore every one must take heed not to intrude himself by improper means, but is bound to wait till it shall please God to call him, and be certain and assured that it is of the Lord.
>
> As for the ministers of God's Word, they have equally the same power and authority wheresoever they are, as they are all ministers of Christ, the only universal Bishop and the only Head of the Church.
>
> Moreover, in order that this holy ordinance of God may not be violated or slighted, we say that every one ought to esteem the ministers of God's Word and the elders of the Church very highly for their work's sake, and be at peace with them without murmuring, strife, or contention, as much as possible.

Reflection Question

Write down any knowledge/thoughts you have about the concept of "a calling."

Study Questions

Who ultimately calls men to be "officers" in the Church?

How does the church go about recognizing that calling?
(1 Tim 3:1–13)

Why is it important to say that all pastors have the same authority?

How many "universal Bishop[s]" are there? Who is he?
(Heb 13:20; 1 Pet 2:25, 5:4)

What do we say about the Pope or anyone else who claims to be *the* pastor of the Church?

I confidently affirm that whoever calls himself *sacerdos universalis*, or desires to be so called by others is in his pride a forerunner of Antichrist.[2]

Church Authority

In article 32, "Of the Power of the Church in Establishing Ecclesiastical Laws and in Administering Discipline," we confess the authority that the elders of the local church have in establishing worship practices and exercising church discipline. It is an explanation, therefore, of the third mark of the true church—discipline. Discipline is a beneficial and pastoral act that Christ commands us to observe:

> In the meantime we believe, though it is useful and beneficial that those who are rulers of the Church institute and establish certain ordinances among themselves for maintaining the body of the Church, yet that they ought studiously to take care that they do not depart from those things which Christ, our only Master, has instituted. And therefore we reject all human inventions, and all laws which man would introduce into the worship of God, thereby to bind and compel the conscience in any manner whatever. Therefore we admit only of that which tends to nourish and preserve concord and unity, and to keep all men in obedience to God. For this purpose, excommunication or church discipline is requisite, with all that pertains to it, according to the Word of God.

Heidelberg Catechism, Q&A 83

> What is the Office of the Keys?
>
> The preaching of the Holy Gospel and Christian discipline; by these two the kingdom of heaven is opened to believers and shut against unbelievers.

Heidelberg Catechism, Q&A 85

> How is the kingdom of heaven shut and opened by Christian discipline?
>
> In this way: that, according to the command of Christ, if any under the Christian name show themselves unsound either in doctrine or

---

[2] St. Gregory the Great; cited in *Cambridge Medieval History*, section written by W.H. Hutton, ed. H.M. Gwatkin and J.P. Whitney (NY: MacMillan, 1967) II:247.

in life, and after several brotherly admonitions do not turn from their errors or evil ways, they are complained of to the Church or to its proper officers; and, if they neglect to hear them also, are by them denied the holy sacraments and thereby excluded from the Christian communion, and by God Himself from the kingdom of Christ; and if they promise and show real amendment, they are again received as members of Christ and His Church.

Reflection Question

In your own words, how much authority does the church have?

Study Questions

How are the pastors and elders to decide how the Church is to worship? (Matt 28:20; *Heidelberg Catechism*, Q&A 96–98)

What is an example of something "which binds and compels" the conscience of Christians in worship?

What is the purpose of church discipline and excommunication? (*Heidelberg Catechism*, Q&A 83, 85) Is it necessary?

For Further Study

On the duties of ministers see Daniel Hyde, "The True Christian Minister." *The Presbyterian Banner* (September 2003): 56.

On the duties of elders see Daniel Hyde, "The Duties of Elders." *Ordained Servant* 13:1 (January 2004): 4–7.

On *Belgic Confession* article 30 see Daniel Hyde, "We Confess: Article 30." *The Outlook* 56:2 (February 2006): 5–9.

On *Belgic Confession* article 31 see Daniel Hyde, "We Confess: Article 31." *The Outlook* 56:3 (March 2006): 7–11.

On *Belgic Confession* article 32 see Daniel Hyde, "We Confess: Article 32." *The Outlook* 56:4 (April 2006): 8–11.

16

The Sacraments

Reflection Question

How do you know that God is gracious to you?

As we confessed in article 29, we distinguish a true church from a false church by three marks. Here in articles 33–35 we have our confession about the second mark of the true church—the pure administration of the sacraments. Article 33 is an explanation of the Reformed understanding of the nature of the sacraments—what a sacrament is, what a sacrament does, and how many sacraments there are in Scripture.

The Idea of Sacraments

Article 33, "Of the Sacraments," says,

> We believe that our gracious God, taking account of our weakness and infirmities, has ordained the sacraments for us, thereby to seal unto us His promises, and to be pledges of the good will and grace of God towards us, and also to nourish and strengthen our faith; which He has joined to the Word of the gospel, the better to present to our senses both that which He declares to us by His Word and that which He works in our hearts, thereby confirming in us the salvation which He imparts to us. For they are visible signs and seals of an inward and invisible thing, by means whereof God works in us by the power of the Holy Spirit. Therefore the signs are not empty or meaningless, so as to deceive us. For Jesus Christ is the true object presented by them, without whom they would be of no moment.

The Good Confession

Moreover, we are satisfied with the number of sacraments which Christ our Lord has instituted, which are two only, namely, the sacrament of baptism and the holy supper of our Lord Jesus Christ.

Heidelberg Catechism, Q&A 65

Since, then, we are made partakers of Christ and all His benefits by faith only, where does this faith come from? The Holy Spirit works faith in our hearts by the preaching of the Holy Gospel, and confirms it by the use of the holy sacraments.

Study Questions

Define "sacrament" in your own words.

Why do we call them "signs?" (Gen 17:11)

Why do we call them "seals?" (Rom 4:11)

Why are sacraments necessary?
(*Heidelberg Catechism*, Q&A 65)

What do the sacraments do?

The Sacraments

What do the sacraments do better than the preached Word?

> Why do we answer the question, "How many sacraments has Christ instituted in the New Testament," by saying, "Two: Holy Baptism and the Holy Supper?"
> (*Heidelberg Catechism*, Q&A 68)

Baptism

Baptism is itself a dramatic portrayal of the death and resurrection of Christ as well as the outpouring of his Holy Spirit upon the Church. In one of the longest and most interesting articles in our *Confession*, article 34, "Of Baptism," describes the Reformed view of baptism. Baptism is the sign of initiation into the covenant community, replacing Old Testament circumcision:

> We believe and confess that Jesus Christ, who is the end of the law, has made, by the shedding of His blood, of all other sheddings of blood which men could or would make as a propitiation or satisfaction for sin; and that He, having abolished circumcision, which was done with blood, has instituted the sacrament of baptism instead thereof; by which we are received into the Church of God, and separated from all other people and strange religions, that we may wholly belong to Him whose mark and ensign we bear; and which serves as a testimony to us that He will be our gracious God and Father.
>
> Therefore He has commanded all those who are His to be baptized with pure water, *into the name of the Father and of the Son and of the Holy Spirit*, thereby signifying to us, that as water washes away the filth of the body when poured upon it, and is seen on the body of the baptized when sprinkled upon him, so does the blood of Christ by the power of the Holy Spirit internally sprinkle the soul, cleanse it from its sins, and regenerate us from children of wrath unto children of God. Not that this is effected by the external water, but by the sprinkling of the precious blood of the Son of God; who is our Red Sea, through which we must pass to

escape the tyranny of Pharaoh, that is, the devil, and to enter into the spiritual land of Canaan.

The ministers, therefore, on their part administer the sacrament and that which is visible, but our Lord gives that which is signified by the sacrament, namely, the gifts and invisible grace; washing, cleansing, and purging our souls of all filth and unrighteousness; renewing our hearts and filling them with all comfort; giving unto us a true assurance of His fatherly goodness; putting on us the new man, and putting off the old man with all his deeds.

We believe, therefore, that every man who is earnestly studious of obtaining life eternal ought to be baptized but once with this only baptism, without ever repeating the same, since we cannot be born twice. Neither does this baptism avail us only at the time when the water is poured upon us and received by us, but also through the whole course of our life.

Therefore we detest the error of the Anabaptists, who are not content with the one only baptism they have received, and moreover condemn the baptism of the infants of believers, who we believe ought to be baptized and sealed with the sign of the covenant, as the children in Israel formerly were circumcised upon the same promises which are made unto our children. And indeed Christ shed His blood no less for the washing of the children of believers than for adult persons; and therefore they ought to receive the sign and sacrament of which Christ has done for them; as the Lord commanded in the law that they should be made partakers of the sacrament of Christ's suffering and death shortly after they were born, by offering for them a lamb, which was a sacrament of Jesus Christ. Moreover, what circumcision was to the Jews, baptism is to our children. And for this reason St. Paul calls baptism the *circumcision of Christ*.

Heidelberg Catechism, Q&A 69

How is it signified and sealed to you in Holy Baptism that you have part in the one sacrifice of Christ on the cross?

Thus: that Christ instituted this outward washing with water and joined to it this promise, that I am washed with His blood and Spirit from the pollution of my soul, that is, from all my sins, as certainly as I am washed outwardly with water, whereby commonly the filthiness of the body is taken away.

Heidelberg Catechism, Q&A 70

What is it to be washed with the blood and Spirit of Christ?

The Sacraments

It is to have the forgiveness of sins from God through grace, for the sake of Christ's blood, which He shed for us in His sacrifice on the cross; and also to be renewed by the Holy Spirit and sanctified to be members of Christ, so that we may more and more die unto sin and lead holy and unblamable lives.

Heidelberg Catechism, Q&A 71

Where has Christ promised that we are as certainly washed with His blood and Spirit as with the water of Baptism?

In the institution of Baptism, which says: "Go therefore, and teach all nations, baptizing them in the name of the Father, and of the Son, and of the Holy Spirit. He that believes and is baptized shall be saved; but he that believes not shall be damned." This promise is also repeated where Scripture calls Baptism the washing of regeneration and the washing away of sins.

Heidelberg Catechism, Q&A 72

Is, then, the outward washing with water itself the washing away of sins?

No, for only the blood of Jesus Christ and the Holy Spirit cleanse us from all sin.

Heidelberg Catechism, Q&A 73

Why then does the Holy Spirit call Baptism the washing of regeneration and the washing away of sins?

God speaks thus with great cause, namely, not only to teach us thereby that just as the filthiness of the body is taken away by water, so our sins are taken away by the blood and Spirit of Christ; but much more, that by this divine pledge and token He may assure us that we are as really washed from our sins spiritually as our bodies are washed with water.

Heidelberg Catechism, Q&A 74

Are infants also to be baptized?

Yes, for since they, as well as their parents, belong to the covenant and people of God, and through the blood of Christ both redemption from sin and the Holy Spirit, who works faith, are promised to them no less than to their parents, they are also by Baptism, as a sign of the covenant, to be ingrafted into the Christian Church, and distinguished from the children of unbelievers, as was done in the Old Testament by circumcision, in place of which in the New Testament Baptism is appointed.

Reflection Question

In what kinds of rites/ceremonies do we participate as people (e.g., Americans, parents, husbands/wives)

Study Questions

What is the theological reason why circumcision involved blood? Why does baptism not involve blood?

What did circumcision do that baptism also does? (Gen 17:9–14; Exod 11:7; 1 Cor 7:14)

What do you think the *Confession* means when it says we are to be baptized with "plain water?"

What is the *sign* in baptism?

The Sacraments

What is *signified* in baptism? (1 Cor 10:1–2)

What is the analogy the *Confession* gives between ordinary water and baptismal water?

What are some of the Old Testament "types" (a type is an Old Testament preview of something in the New) of baptism?

Does the mode (i.e., immersion, sprinkling, pouring) of baptism make a baptism true?

How many times should we be baptized? Why? (John 3)

The *Confession* speaks of the lifelong benefits of baptism, saying, "Neither does this baptism avail us only at the time when the water is poured upon us and received by us, but also through the whole course of our life." Explain how a one-time sacrament can benefit us for life.

The Good Confession
Why do we baptize children of Christians?[1]

The Lord's Supper

The Lord's Supper (also called Holy Communion or the Eucharist) is a dramatic portrayal of the death of our Lord Jesus Christ and is the sacrament of nourishment. One of the greatest controversies during the Reformation between the Roman Catholics and Protestants as well as among the Protestants themselves (Reformed, Lutherans, and Zwinglians) was over the Lord's Supper. There is much confusion, although there should not be. The Reformed view expressed here in the *Belgic Confession* (which is also the view of John Calvin) is very simple, yet mysterious. This article is the greatest summary statement of the Reformed view in all confessional literature. Article 35, "Of the Lord's Supper," says,

> We believe and confess that our Savior Jesus Christ did ordain and institute the sacrament of the holy supper to nourish and support those whom He has already regenerated and incorporated into His family, which is His Church.
>
> Now those who are regenerated have in them a twofold life, the one corporal and temporal, which they have from the first birth and is common to all men; the other spiritual and heavenly, which is given them in their second birth, which is effected by the Word of the gospel, in the communion of the body of Christ; and this life is not common, but is peculiar to God's elect. In like manner God has given us, for the support of the bodily and earthly life, earthly and common bread, which is subservient thereto and is common to all men, even as life itself. But for the support of the spiritual and heavenly life which believers have He has sent a living bread, which descended from heaven, namely, Jesus Christ, who nourishes and strengthens the spiritual life of believers when they eat Him, that is to say, when they appropriate and receive Him by faith in the spirit.
>
> In order that He might represent unto us this spiritual and heavenly bread, Christ has instituted earthly and visible bread as a sacrament of His body, and wine as a sacrament of His blood,

---

[1] See Daniel R. Hyde, *Jesus Loves the Little Children: Why We Baptize Children* Granville: Reformed Fellowship, 2006).

to testify by them unto us that, as certainly as we receive and hold this sacrament in our hands and eat and drink the same with our mouths, by which our life is afterwards nourished, we also do as certainly receive by faith (which is the hand and mouth of our soul) the true body and blood of Christ our only Savior, in our souls, for the support of our spiritual life.

Now, as it is certain and beyond all doubt that Jesus Christ has not enjoined to us the use of His sacraments in vain, so He works in us all that He represents to us by these holy signs, though the manner surpasses our understanding and cannot be comprehended by us, as the operations of the Holy Spirit are hidden and incomprehensible. In the meantime we err not when we say that what is eaten and drunk by us is the proper and natural body and the proper blood of Christ. But the manner of our partaking of the same is not by the mouth, but by the spirit through faith. Thus, then, though Christ always sits at the right hand of His Father in the heavens, yet does He not therefore cease to make us partakers of Himself by faith. This feast is a spiritual table, at which Christ communicates Himself with all His benefits to us, and gives us there to enjoy both Himself and the merits of His sufferings and death: nourishing, strengthening, and comforting our poor comfortless souls by the eating of His flesh, quickening and refreshing them by the drinking of His blood.

Further, though the sacraments are connected with the thing signified nevertheless both are not received by all men. The ungodly indeed receives the sacrament to his condemnation, but he does not receive the truth of the sacrament, even as Judas and Simon the sorcerer both indeed received the sacrament not Christ who was signified by it, of whom believers only are made partakers.

Lastly, we receive this holy sacrament in the assembly of the people of God, with humility and reverence, keeping up among us a holy remembrance of the death of Christ our Savior, with thanksgiving, making confession of our faith and of the Christian religion. Therefore no one ought to come to this table without having previously rightly examined himself, lest by eating of this bread and drinking of this cup he eat and drink judgment to himself. In a word, we are moved by the use of this holy sacrament to a fervent love of God and our neighbor.

Therefore we reject all mixtures and damnable inventions which men have added unto and blended with the sacraments, as profanations of them; and affirm that we ought to rest satisfied with the ordinance which Christ and His apostles have taught us, and that we must speak of them in the same manner as they have spoken.

Heidelberg Catechism, Q&A 75

How is it signified and sealed to you in the Holy Supper that you partake of the one sacrifice of Christ on the cross and all His benefits?

Thus: that Christ has commanded me and all believers to eat of this broken bread and to drink of this cup in remembrance of Him, and has joined therewith these promises: first, that His body was offered and broken on the cross for me and His blood shed for me, as certainly as I see with my eyes the bread of the Lord broken for me and the cup communicated to me; and further, that with His crucified body and shed blood He Himself feeds and nourishes my soul to everlasting life, as certainly as I receive from the hand of the minister and taste with my mouth the bread and cup of the Lord, which are given me as certain tokens of the body and blood of Christ.

Heidelberg Catechism, Q&A 76

What does it mean to eat the crucified body and drink the shed blood of Christ?

It means not only to embrace with a believing heart all the sufferings and death of Christ, and thereby to obtain the forgiveness of sins and life eternal; but moreover, also, to be so united more and more to His sacred body by the Holy Spirit, who dwells both in Christ and in us, that, although He is in heaven and we on earth, we are nevertheless flesh of His flesh and bone of His bone, and live and are governed forever by one Spirit, as members of the same body are governed by one soul.

Heidelberg Catechism, Q&A 77

Where has Christ promised that He will thus feed and nourish believers with His body and blood as certainly as they eat of this broken bread and drink of this cup?

In the institution of the Supper, which says: *"The Lord Jesus the same night in which He was betrayed took bread: and when He had given thanks, He broke it, and said, Take, eat: this is my body, which is broken for you: this do in remembrance of me. After the same manner also He took the cup, when He had eaten, saying, This cup is the new covenant in my blood: this do, as often as you drink it, in remembrance of me. For as often as you eat this bread, and drink this cup, you proclaim the Lord's death till He come."* And this promise is also repeated by the Apostle Paul, where he says: *"The cup of blessing which we bless, is it not the communion of the blood of Christ? The bread which we break, is it not the communion of the body of Christ? Because there is one bread, so we being many are one body, for we are all partakers of that one bread."*

Heidelberg Catechism, Q&A 78

Do, then, the bread and the wine become the real body and blood of Christ?

No, but as the water in Baptism is not changed into the blood of Christ, nor becomes the washing away of sins itself, being only the divine token and assurance thereof, so also in the Lord's Supper the sacred bread does not become the body of Christ itself, though agreeably to the nature and usage of sacraments it is called the body of Christ.

Heidelberg Catechism, Q&A 79

Why then does Christ call the bread His body, and the cup His blood, or the new covenant in His blood; and the apostle Paul, the communion of the body and the blood of Christ?

Christ speaks thus with great cause, namely, not only to teach us thereby, that like as the bread and wine sustain this temporal life, so also His crucified body and shed blood are the true meat and drink of our souls unto life eternal; but much more, by this visible sign and pledge to assure us that we are as really partakers of His true body and blood by the working of the Holy Spirit, as we receive by the mouth of the body these holy tokens in remembrance of Him; and that all His sufferings and obedience are as certainly our own, as if we ourselves had suffered and done all in our own person.

Heidelberg Catechism, Q&A 80

What difference is there between the Lord's Supper and the Pope's Mass?

The Lord's Supper testifies to us that we have full forgiveness of all our sins by the one sacrifice of Jesus Christ, which He Himself once accomplished on the cross; and that by the Holy Spirit we are ingrafted into Christ, who, with His true body, is now in heaven at the right hand of the Father, and is there to be worshipped. But the Mass teaches that the living and the dead do not have forgiveness of sins through the sufferings of Christ, unless Christ is still daily offered for them by the priests, and that Christ is bodily under the form of bread and wine, and is therefore to be worshipped in them. And thus the Mass at bottom is nothing else than a denial of the one sacrifice and suffering of Jesus Christ, and an accursed idolatry.

Reflection Question

The *Confession* here says that we have a "twofold life," meaning, a physical and spiritual life. How important is eating and drinking for both?

Study Questions

There are four (4) major views of the Lord's Supper. Can you list them?

1.   (Roman Catholicism)

2.   (Lutheranism)

3.   (Zwinglianism/Evangelicalism)

4.   (Reformed—sorry, no "ism!")

There are various biblical names for the Lord's Supper. Next to each, write down what you think that name says about this sacrament:

1. Lord's Supper (1 Cor 11:20)—

The Sacraments

2. Communion (1 Cor 10:16)—

3. Lord's Table (1 Cor 10:21)—

4. Eucharist (1 Cor 10:16)—

5. Breaking of the bread (Acts 2:42)—

The *Confession* gives an analogy between ordinary bread and the Lord's Supper. What does this tell us about the purpose of the Lord's Supper?

What is the *sign* of the Lord's Supper?

What is the thing *signified* by the Supper? (Matt 26:26)

How do we receive and eat the body and blood of Christ?

Can we comprehend how we commune with the "true, proper, and natural" body and blood of Christ? Is it Roman Catholic to say, "what we eat and drink is the true, natural body and the true blood of Christ?" (1 Cor 10:16) Why or why not?

Where is Christ's human nature? (*Heidelberg Catechism*, Q&A 46–49) Why is that important for our understanding of the Supper?

Who may partake of the Lord's Supper? (see below)

Heidelberg Catechism, Q&A 81

Who are to come to the table of the Lord?

Those who are displeased with themselves for their sins, yet trust that these are forgiven them, and that their remaining infirmity is covered by the suffering and death of Christ; who also desire more and more to strengthen their faith and to amend their life. But the impenitent and hypocrites eat and drink judgment to themselves.

Heidelberg Catechism, Q&A 82

Are they, then, also to be admitted to this Supper who show themselves by their confession and life to be unbelieving and ungodly?

No, for thereby the covenant of God is profaned and His wrath provoked against the whole congregation; therefore, the Christian Church is bound, according to the order of Christ and His Apostles, to exclude such persons by the Office of the Keys until they amend their lives.

For Further Study

On *Belgic Confession* article 33, see Daniel Hyde, "We Confess: Article 33" *The Outlook* 56:5 (May 2006): 10–14.

On *Belgic Confession* article 34, see Daniel Hyde, "We Confess: Article 34" *The Outlook* 56:6 (June 2006): 10–14.

On *Belgic Confession* article 35, see Daniel Hyde, "We Confess: Article 35" *The Outlook* 56:7 (July/August 2006): 12-15.

On the subject of the sacraments see Horton, *Putting Amazing Back Into Grace*, 161–180 and "Mysteries of God and Means of Grace." *Modern Reformation* (May/June 1997): 3–14.

On the topic of baptism see W. Robert Godfrey, "Why Baptism?" *Modern Reformation* (May/June 1997): 27–31.

On the subject of the Lord's Supper see R. Scott Clark, "The Evangelical Fall From the Means of Grace: The Lord's Supper," in *The Compromised Church* (Wheaton: Crossway, 1998), 133–47 and W. Robert Godfrey, "Calvin on the Eucharist," *Modern Reformation* 6:3 (May/June 1997): 48–50.

17

The Return of Christ and Heaven

REFLECTION QUESTION

Reflect upon the fact that our Confession has one article on "the end times" while modern-day Christians emphasize it so much as to have best-sellers on this topic.

OUR DRAMA reaches its conclusion as we come from creation, fall, and redemption to the consummation. As we come to this final scene, we see that our dogmatic drama as presented by the *Belgic Confession* begins with God (art. 1) and ends with God (art. 37). He is the Alpha and the Omega of biblical revelation. As we confess the doctrine of the end (*eschatology*), notice that the *Confession* spends only one of its thirty-seven articles on "the end times," contrary to much modern-day end times fascination. This reminds us to keep our discussion of the end in perspective.

The Last Things

Article 37, "Of the Last Judgment, Resurrection of the Body, and Eternal Life," explains what we believe about the Second Coming of Christ in simple, biblical terms: Jesus Christ shall conclude human history at the last judgment and thereby usher in the final state in a renewed heavens and earth:

> Finally, we believe, according to the Word of God, when the time appointed by the Lord (which is unknown to all creatures) is come and the number of the elect complete, that our Lord Jesus Christ will come from heaven, corporally and visibly, as He ascended, with great glory and majesty to declare Himself Judge of the liv-

ing and the dead, burning this old world with fire and flame to cleanse it.

Then all men will personally appear before this great Judge, both men and women and children, that have been from the beginning of the world to the end thereof, being summoned by *the voice of the archangel, and by the sound of the trump of God*. For all the dead shall be raised out of the earth, and their souls joined and united with their proper bodies in which they formerly lived. As for those who shall then be living, they shall not die as the others, but be changed in the twinkling of an eye, and from corruptible become incorruptible, Then *the books* (that is to say, the consciences) *shall be opened, and the dead judged* according to what they have done in this world, whether it be good or evil. Nay, all men *shall give account of every idle word they have spoken*, which the world counts amusement and jest; and then the secrets and hypocrisy of men shall be disclosed and laid open before all.

And therefore the consideration of this judgment is justly terrible and dreadful to the wicked and ungodly, but most desirable and comfortable to the righteous and elect; because then their full deliverance shall be perfected, and there they shall receive the fruits of their labor and trouble which they have borne. Their innocence shall be known to all, and they shall see the terrible vengeance which God shall execute on the wicked, who most cruelly persecuted, oppressed, and tormented them in this world, and who shall be convicted by the testimony of their own consciences, and shall become immortal, but only to be tormented in *the eternal fire which is prepared for the devil and his angels*.

But on the contrary, the faithful and elect shall be crowned with glory and honor; and the Son of God will confess their names before God His Father and His elect angels; all tears shall be wiped from their eyes; and their cause which is now condemned by many judges and magistrates as heretical and impious will then be known to be the cause of the Son of God. And for a gracious reward, the Lord will cause them to possess such a glory as never entered into the heart of man to conceive.

Therefore we expect that great day with a most ardent desire, to the end that we may fully enjoy the promises of God in Christ Jesus our Lord. AMEN.

Amen, come, Lord Jesus. (Rev 22:20)

Heidelberg Catechism, Q&A 52

What comfort is it to you that Christ "shall come to judge the living and the dead?"

The Return of Christ and Heaven

That in all my sorrows and persecutions, I, with uplifted head, look for the very One, who offered Himself for me to the judgment of God, and removed all curse from me, to come as Judge from heaven, who shall cast all His and my enemies into everlasting condemnation, but shall take me with all His chosen ones to Himself into heavenly joy and glory.

STUDY QUESTIONS

What does the word "eschatology" mean?

List the major views of eschatology that you know of below:

When is Christ coming again?

What will happen when he returns?

How many times is he going to return?

Do Reformed Christians believe in a "rapture?"
Why or why not?

What will happen to the heavens and earth when Christ returns? (2 Pet 3:5–7, 10–13; Rev 21–22)

What does the Second Coming cause in us?

How is the *Belgic Confession's* explanation of the "last days" different from what you may have previously learned?

For Further Study

On *Belgic Confession* article 37, see Daniel Hyde, "We Confess: Article 37." *The Outlook* 56:9 (October 2006): 21-24.

For a basic explanation of Reformed, amillennial eschatology, see Horton, *Putting Amazing Back Into Grace*, 181–202; Kim Riddlebarger, *A Case for Amillennialism* (Grand Rapids: Baker, 2003); Robert B. Strimple, "Amillennialism," in *Three Views on the Millennium and Beyond*, ed. Darrell L. Bock (Grand Rapids: Zondervan, 1999) 83–129; Anthony A. Hoekema, *The Bible and the Future* (Grand Rapids: Eerdmans, 1979); Cornelis P. Venema, *The Promise of the Future* (Edinburgh: Banner of Truth, 2000); Geerhardus Vos, *The Pauline Eschatology* (Phillipsburg: P&R, reprinted 1994); O.T. Allis, *Prophecy and the Church* (Phillipsburg: Presbyterian & Reformed, 1947).

The three great Reformed, amillennial commentaries on the book of Revelation, from simplest to most difficult are: William Hendricksen, *More Than Conquerors* (7th printing; Grand Rapids: Baker, 1990); Dennis E. Johnson, *The Triumph of the Lamb* (Phillipsburg: P&R, 2001); G.K. Beale, *The Book of Revelation* (NIGTC; Grand Rapids: Eerdmans, 1999). For a basic guide to reading the book of Revelation, see Daniel Hyde, "How Do I Read the Book of Revelation?" *The Presbyterian Banner* (July 2004): 3–4.

18

Understanding and Enjoying Worship

To worship is to quicken the conscience by the holiness of God, to purge the imagination by the beauty of God, to open the heart to the love of God, and to devote the will to the purpose of God.
(William Temple)

Reflection Question

Is worship a matter of personal style and taste?
Do you think the Bible actually dictates not only
the God who is to be worshipped, but *how*?

Many of us have recently come to Reformed churches from a myriad of church backgrounds and styles. The experience goes a little something like this, right? The biblical teaching that God sovereignly and eternally elected you without any regard to your works, goodness, or decision confronts you. Then comes Christ's atoning work for those whom the Father has given him, the effectual power and calling of the Holy Spirit of those elect and died-for-ones, and then comes their preservation and perseverance in grace until they reach glory.

Where do you go to church, though? All you know is Maranatha! Music™, contemporary style services and fellowships. The idea of "traditional," cold services in with a "liturgy" is not your cup of tea nor was it your intention when you submitted to God's Word on the above doctrines.

The purpose of this chapter is to explain to you why we as Reformed churches worship the way we do, whether you come from a non-Reformed background or whether you are a veteran of Reformed worship. To understand historic Reformed, and we think, biblical, worship is to understand God himself and our response to his grace to us in Christ. Reformed worship is passionate, led by the Holy Spirit, and glorifying to our Father in heaven.

What is a Liturgy?

"Liturgy" is almost a four-letter word among some Christians today. But, in fact, our English word "liturgy" comes from an ancient Greek word for "service." From this Greek word we get the simple meaning and idea of "an order of worship."

Every church, therefore, uses a liturgy. It is not something only a few churches have, such as the Roman Catholics or "traditional" churches; every worship service in every church the world has a liturgy. Whether or not a particular church has a more structured or loose service, or whether a "liturgy" is printed in the bulletin and followed or not, does not make one church liturgical and another not, as all have a liturgy every time there is worship. Anyone who thinks that a particular church gathers and is led by the Spirit through the praise band is unfortunately mistaken.

What we must ask ourselves, as Christians seeking to worship the Father in "spirit and truth" is not whether we have a liturgy, but since we have one, let us put it in the light of Scripture to see whether it is biblical or not.

As Reformed churches we follow the cry of the Reformers, "Reformed according to Scripture." Our Protestant forefathers did not "throw the baby out with the bath water," but went "back to the sources" (Latin, *ad fontes*) of Scripture; they also looked to the ancient church's liturgies as testimonies of Scripture's truths (Latin, *testes veritas*). The Reformers stripped the Medieval Mass of its idolatry and extra-Scriptural content; they did not re-invent the wheel. Therefore, what you experience as you worship with a Reformed church is a fully biblical service in the same vein as the historic liturgies of the ancient church, which were revived during the 16th century Protestant Reformation by the Reformers. We hope to communicate these eternal principles of God's Word, as passed down through the centuries, in a meaningful way to a 21st century world. It is not our desire simply to reproduce old tradition for the sake of being traditional, but we seek to be always Reformed, always Reforming.

Understanding and Enjoying Worship

Reflection Question

What is the "liturgy" to which you are accustomed?
(Write it our below)

Who Decides What is Placed in the Liturgy?

The particular elements, or things that we do, in the order of worship are clearly commanded to us by God himself or deduced by solid principles of interpretation from the inspired Word of God, "by which we may serve God acceptably with reverence and godly fear" (Heb 12:28). We call this the "Regulative Principle;" that is, God through his Word regulates how we are to worship. This is the meaning of the Second Commandment. The one true God who has commanded us to worship him alone (First Commandment) also tells us the way we are to do this (Second Commandment).

This also brings to mind the principle of the sufficiency of Scripture. God's Word is sufficient, for it alone is our guide for teaching, theology, and doctrine, and living, practice, and life. Therefore, if his Word is sufficient for our salvation and Christian life then it surely is all we need in order to worship him as he desires and deserves. Since we seek to please an audience of one, our Triune God, it is only when worshipping according to how he wants to be worshipped that our worship is pleasing to him. Therefore, God decides what is placed in the corporate service of worship. Jesus Christ alone is the only "worship leader" of his Church as Psalm 22:22–26 so beautifully states for us.

What is Placed in the Liturgy?

The acceptable elements of the worship of the Triune God are, broadly speaking, elements of the Word, the Sacraments, and Prayer (Acts 2:42).[1]

---

[1] This is the traditional Reformed division, following John Calvin, who said in his *Preface to the Psalter*, "Now there are briefly three things which our Lord commanded us to observe in our spiritual assemblies: namely, the preaching of His Word, prayers public and solemn, and the administration of the sacraments."

Word

Under the Word there is the call to worship (ex: Ps 95), the reading of the Law/Scripture and preaching of the Word of God (1 Tim 4:13), the absolution/declaration of pardon after the reading of the Law (1 John 1:9; Matt 18:18; John 20:23), and God's greeting (Rev 1:4–5) and benediction (Num 6:24–26; 2 Cor 13:14).

Sacraments

Under the sacraments, there is the administration of Baptism and the Lord's Supper according to Christ's commands (Luke 22:17–20; 1 Cor 11:23–26).

Prayer

Under the element of prayer, we distinguish two kinds: spoken prayer and sung prayer.[2] The spoken prayers are the plethora of Scriptural types of prayers: the pastoral prayer (1 Tim 2:1), confession (Ps 51), and adoration (Ps 8). Under sung prayers is congregational singing, especially of the inspired hymnbook of the covenant people, the Psalms (Eph 5:19; Col 3:16).

In the history of the Reformed churches, we have been primarily and principally Psalm-singing churches. For example, the *Church Order of the Synod of Dort* (1618–19), article 69, says

> In the Churches only the 150 Psalms of David, the Ten Commandments, the Lord's Prayer, the Twelve Articles of Faith, the Song of Mary, that of Zacharius, and that of Simeon shall be sung. It is left to the individual Churches whether or not to use the hymn, "Oh God! who art our Father." All other hymns are to be excluded from the Churches, and in those places where some have already been introduced, they are to be removed by the most suitable means.[3]

Later in 1934, article 69 was changed by the Christian Reformed Church (the roots of the URCNA) to say

> In the churches only the 150 Psalms of David and the collection of hymns for church use, approved and adopted by synod, shall be sung. However, *while the singing of the psalms is a divine re-*

---

[2] Calvin, *Preface to the Psalter*.
[3] As found in *The Psalter* (Grand Rapids: Reformation Heritage Books, 1999), 187.

quirement, the use of the approved hymns is left to the freedom of the churches.[4] (Emphasis mine)

Finally, the current *Church Order of the United Reformed Churches in North America*, article 39, says,

> The 150 Psalms *shall* have the principal place in the singing of the churches. Hymns which faithfully and fully reflect the teaching of the Scripture as expressed in the Three Forms of Unity *may* be sung, provided they are approved by the Consistory. (Emphasis mine)

Reflection Question

Think back to other churches you may have attended and/or been a member of. What else was included in the worship service? Is there biblical support for it?

Why Is the Reformed Liturgy Structured the Way It Is?

Our worship is a reflection of our theology, and our theology must reflect in our worship. What the Scriptures reveal about God, salvation, and us must be evident in our worship. As well, how we worship is a window into what we believe about God, us, and how God saves us.

Following are some basic theological principles that guide our worship. First, the Bible is clear in teaching that our God is a sovereign, covenant-making God. The God who called us into being and who has called us to faith is the same God who calls us to worship. This sovereign, almighty God has done all this through the means of covenants. He created, then came to the rescue after man's fall into sin by beginning the covenant of grace in Genesis 3:15, and guided his people through history to the climax of redemption: Jesus Christ.

Second, it is because of our sin and depravity, God always initiates worship because we never would apart from his Spirit calling us to do so.

---

[4] *Psalter Hymnal* (Grand Rapids: Christian Reformed Church, 1934), 124.

This is why we hold dearly the words of the Psalmist: "O LORD open my lips, and my mouth shall show forth Your praise" (Ps 51:15; NKLV).

Third, God not only initiates, but also condescends to us in our worship. He stoops down to us in order to raise us to him. He stoops to us in the means of grace, the preaching of the Gospel (audible Word) and administration of the sacraments (visible Word).

Thus Reformed worship reflects the Scriptural teachings of God's sovereignty and holiness, our horrible blindness in sin, and God's condescending to us in grace and mercy.

Therefore we do not call our worship either "traditional" nor "contemporary" worship, but "covenantal worship." Just as in covenants, one side speaks and the other responds, so too in worship there is this dialog between our great God who speaks to us in grace and our response to him in gratitude. So we also speak of worship as guided by the "dialogical principle."

Because of this our service is not structured after nineteenth century revivalism in which there is an extended period of "worship" (the time of singing), then the message, and then the altar call (a substitute for the sacrament of the Lord's Supper); but our service transcends all cultures, times, and peoples as it is biblically structured. This is why we have the "call-response" structure or style, in which the minister, in the place and name of Christ, calls us out of the world to worship the heavenly King, then we respond in praise, God greets us, and we extol his marvelous name. God then speaks his Law and we response in humble confession of our many sins; but God speaks his pardon in Christ and we exclaim with thanksgiving. He then speaks his preached Word, and we respond in prayer and offering; finally, God has the final word as he does the first, with his blessing as we depart to serve him.

What Is the Purpose of a Biblically Reformed Liturgy?

First, by placing an abundance of Scripture before us, a Reformed liturgy focuses our minds and hearts upon the glory of God in Christ, while taking our minds off ourselves. The Reformation slogan, echoing Romans 11:33–36, of "to God alone be the glory" is our driving goal in worship.

Second, a biblical liturgy gets our focus off this world and onto the hope of the next. In an age of the microwave mentality, the sound byte, headline news, and a consumer society, Reformed churches gather on the Lord's Day. We do this to set aside our six days of labor, of worry, and of anxiety in order to participate in something that is larger than us, that has been around longer than us, and that fills our hearts with true fulfillment.

Third, the liturgy calls us to participate actively and not to be an observer. We are not watching a priest do all the work—we are the priests. Worship is also not a time of entertainment in which we sit back and enjoy, but a time of entering the very presence of God himself.

Fourth, it shows us the unity of God's redemptive work by tying Old Testament promises and New Testament fulfillment's together.

Fifth, by using an abundance of Scripture, organized in an orderly way, we are reminded and comforted every week that God's Law has been satisfied by the life, death, resurrection, and ascension of Christ, that his righteousness has been imputed to us, that God has graciously pardoned all of our sins, and that he has adopted us as his children.

Explaining the Liturgy

In Reformed churches, we typically follow the basic outline of the liturgy of John Calvin, as he reformed worship in both Strasbourg and Geneva.[5] Below is the basic outline of the order of service Calvin's French speaking congregation used in Strasbourg around the year 1542:

Service of the Word

> Invocation, Psalm 124:8
>
> Confession of Sins
>
> Absolution
>
> Singing of the First Table of God's Commandments
>
> Prayer of Commitment
>
> Singing of the Second Table of God's Commandments
>
> Prayer for Illumination
>
> Scripture Lesson
>
> Sermon
>
> Pastoral Prayer, concluding with the minister's paraphrase of the Lord's Prayer

---

[5] As found in Baird Thompson, *Liturgies of the Western Church* (2nd edition; Philadelphia: Fortress Press, 1982), 197–210

Service of the Lord's Supper

    Singing of the *Apostles' Creed*

    Prayer of Consecration

    The Words of Institution

    Instruction on the Holy Supper

    Distribution of the Elements

    Singing of Psalm 138

    Prayer of Thanksgiving

    Singing of the Song of Simeon

    Benediction, Numbers 6:24–26

Reflection Question

With what elements in the above service are you familiar? What seems different?

Let us now look at a typical order of service for this congregation.[6]

---

[6] The class teacher should here make available this particular church's order of service and explain each part as well as the principles behind why you worship the way you do.

www.ingramcontent.com/pod-product-compliance
Lightning Source LLC
Chambersburg PA
CBHW071448150426
43191CB00008B/1277